MORE
Sheffield
MEMORIES

The publishers would like to thank the following companies for their support in the production of this book

Main Sponsor

Swann-Morton Limited

Atkinsons of Sheffield

Arkote Ltd

Baker Blower

Dexel Tyre Co. Ltd

Fletchers Bakery

Meadowhall

Outokumpu Stainless Ltd

SCX Ltd

Sheffield Forgemasters International

Sheffield Testing Laboratories

Shepherd Distribution Services

Symmetry Medical

University of Sheffield

Wortley Hall

First published in Great Britain by True North Books Limited
England HX3 6AE
01422 344344

ISBN 1 903204 91 7

Text, design and origination by True North Books
Printed and bound by The Amadeus Press

MORE *Sheffield* MEMORIES

CONTENTS

INTRODUCTION

Welcome to 'More Sheffield Memories', the latest in a series of True North books that takes readers back in time to the days of the last century and, quite literally, into an earlier millennium. We all know that the world beyond us, as well the immediate environment around us, changes with each passing day. Nowhere can that be better illustrated than by the stunning and thought provoking images within these pages. Complemented by informative and, at times, wry captions, the photographs show the changes in architecture, fashion, entertainment and transport as each successive generation is visited. These evolving subjects also impacted upon the way we conducted ourselves and regarded others during that timescale. In the earliest photographs women are shown at a time when they could not even vote for the men who were shaping their destiny in Westminster. The motor car was such a remarkable technological rarity that children rushed onto the street to see one. Men, seldom seen without headgear, doffed their caps or bowlers to ladies who went by and grand, individually designed, offices, hotels and shops dominated the city centre view. Looking through the pages of this book you may get an indication of the amount of change that has taken place in Sheffield, and over such a short period, relative to the long history of the area. To put things into perspective, first we need to go back to much

earlier days. Although this is not a history lesson, we need to have some modicum of knowledge of how our city came to its position of standing at the start of the last century. After all, Britain's earliest known house, albeit just a circle of stones in the shape of a hut base, was found at what is now Deepcar, in the north of the city. It is estimated that this find dates back to around 8,000 BC. The origins of Sheffield can be discovered in what was a clearing near the confluence of the Don and Sheaf, from which the city derives its name. However, the first true hard evidence relates to the shaft of an early 9th century stone cross, part of one erected on the future site of Sheffield Cathedral, but removed from the churchyard in 1570. The cross dates from around the time when Vikings were threatening the land and many battles and skirmishes took place during that century. All was to change with the Norman Conquest that began in 1066. By then, Sheffield was starting to take shape. The Domesday Book refers to it as Escafeld or Scafeld. By the 11th century, a Norman baron, William de Lovetot built the wooden Sheffield castle and founded St Mary's Church, Handsworth. A settlement of several hundred grew on the land between the castle and the church and, in addition to agriculture, a small woollen industry was established. A charter giving people the right to hold markets and fairs was granted towards the end of the 13th century, firmly establishing Sheffield as a place of significance.

Even in medieval times, cutlery was one of the trades for which we were noted and, by about 1600, Sheffield was the most prestigious manufacturer outside London. By now, the population had topped 2,000. It continued to grow rapidly over the succeeding years and by 1700 there were 5,000 inhabitants. However, things were to about to move at a

pace never seen before. The industrial revolution was just around the corner. Benjamin Huntsman discovered a way of making a better quality product, crucible steel, and Thomas Bolsover plated copper with silver, providing a cheaper but attractive alternative to solid silver. Sheffield got its own assay office and the town was firmly on the industrial map. During the 19th century, steel production increased in volume and, with the successful work of Henry Bessemer with his steel converter that reduced the cost of manufacture dramatically, steel barons made their millions and workers flocked to the town. Sheffield was incorporated as a Parliamentary borough in 1832, becoming a fully fledged city in 1893. By then, it had nearly 400,000 inhabitants.

Sheffield is the fourth largest city (by area) in England, and a number of its best known and longest established firms have allowed us to access their internal archives. This has enabled us to recount the history of these companies from humble beginnings, in most cases, to leading positions in their chosen area of expertise. These organisations have tremendous social, as well as commercial significance, as between them they represent the places of employment for many thousands of Sheffield people. We are very grateful to the directors of these businesses for their co-operation and valuable support. 'Sweet, sweet the memories you gave to me.' So sang Dean Martin in his famous hit recording of 1956. You are about to go back to that era and beyond on a tour of pure nostalgia for the days of the last century that are precious to all of us. It is time to open a bottle of Ward's finest ale and raise a glass to this trip down memory lane. If we had a modern waitress standing by, serving up a platter of 'More Sheffield Memories', she would now say, 'Enjoy.'

STREET SCENES

Sheffield's original tram system was one of the earliest and most extensive networks in Britain. It was established in 1873 and trams were horse-drawn until 1899, when the first electric routes opened. The system was powered by electricity from then on, with the horse being sent out to grass within a few short years, and routes quickly developed until the new tramway covered the whole city. Seen in the early days of George V's reign, just before the outbreak of the Great War, the trams had already become a common feature of life in and around the city centre. Looking across Fitzalan Square to High Street and Haymarket, we can make out the General Post Office and Birmingham District and Counties Banking Company building. To the right, the Bell Hotel, later to become a gift shop, was a popular hostelry. Horse drawn cabs still looked for custom in the square, attempting to hold off the passage of time that made the tram universally popular. However, there were still sufficient numbers of middle class clients who did not wish to mix with those they regarded as the great unwashed who used public transport. Before long, though, the motor car would provide an alternative form of taxi service. Coincidentally, today finds this part of the city still in use as a centre for modern taxi cabs.

Above: Trams still dominate this part of Sheffield, so the scene today is not very different from this one of the junction of Fitzalan Square and High Street that was taken where the latter changes to Commercial Street. The former Gas Company offices at Bryward House can be seen in the background. Commissioned by the Sheffield United Gas Light Company, the building dates from 1874. Its 131 foot façade was constructed from sandstone and decorated, amongst others, by two stone carved figures either side of the doorway. Sheffield had an extensive network of first-generation trams. The first horse drawn tram ran in 1873 and electric trams began operation in 1899. At its greatest extent, 100 miles of tram routes were operated by Sheffield Corporation. As with all British cities, trams fell out of favour in the 1950s and 60s. Sheffield's last tram ran in 1960, by which time the system was one of only a handful left in Britain. Fitzalan Square reflects one of the family names of the Duke of Norfolk, Lord of the Manor at Handsworth and an influential landowner. Powers to build the square were granted in 1869, but not fully realised until 1881 as a number of dwellings and two public houses had to be demolished. Fitzalan Market Hall stood near this spot from 1786 to 1930.

Below: The Marples Hotel dominated this corner of Fitzalan Square. Its imposing presence dwarfed many of the other buildings around, such as the three storey one belonging to a local firm of nurserymen. Seen in the 1920s, the Marples, or London Mart to give it its proper name, was one of the focal points in the city. We can see just how busy this area was, something of a contrast with today as Fitzalan Square has lost its sense of grandeur and is largely bypassed by modern shoppers and visitors of today because the tramline running down High Street seems to maroon the square. During the interwar years people tried to rebuild their lives after the carnage of the Great War, but life was not easy for the man in the street. The land fit for heroes that Lloyd George promised never materialised and, with jobs in short supply and wages kept at depressed levels, times were tough. They got much worse for this part of the city when the area was heavily bombed in 1940. The Marples was flattened and the site lay as wasteland for many years. John Smith's built a new public house there that opened in 1959 and, for the first time, Marples became its official name. The pub traded right up until the early summer of 2002 when it was suddenly closed. It reopened the following year as a motorcycle accessories' shop.

Below: In 1937, traffic was piling into the city. There were now a number of recent initiatives to make our streets safer places. During this decade, Britain had one of the worst road safety records in the western world for accidents, deaths and injuries. Pro rata it far outweighed modern statistics. A mixture of mass education and legislation was the only way forward. Electrically operated traffic lights were introduced at busy junctions and, where this was not thought to be practicable, roundabouts were created. The Highway Code was published and pedestrian crossings introduced. Remarkably, until 1 June 1935 there was no such thing as a compulsory driving test for anyone getting behind the wheel of a car. Even then, the tests were only given to those who had been driving for less than a year and anyone who could say that he was an experienced driver was almost guaranteed to be given a full licence. It was known that some farmhands whose driving experience was limited to tractors in the fields were granted the right to take a car out without any checks being made. Let us hope that these motorists on Town Hall Square and Fargate, as we look across to the Sheffield Creameries on the corner of Leopold Street, were responsible souls. If not, there was refuge for the pedestrians in the rockery.

Right: Britain celebrated the coronation of George VI on 12 May 1937, the very date that had been earmarked for his brother. However, that plan was tossed into the wastebasket five months earlier when Edward VIII decided that his personal life was more important than the monarchy and abdicated so that he could marry the twice divorced American socialite, Wallis Simpson. But, Westminster Abbey had been booked and the new king decided that he might as well use the reservation for his own official elevation to the throne. Remnants of the celebrations can still be seen in the garlanding of some of the buildings on Haymarket when this scene was captured. Looking from Waingate, named after the wagons that once used this road, Fitzalan Square and the general Post Office can be seen at the top of the photograph. Norfolk Market Hall is on the left. It opened on Christmas Eve 1851, the year of the Great Exhibition at Crystal Palace. Part of the site chosen for the new hall was occupied by the Tontine Inn, whose prosperity was largely dependent on the coaching trade. In 1838 coaches were still leaving, daily to York, Leeds and Birmingham, but the coming of the railways led to a decline in coach services and a reduction in profits. The Tontine was demolished in 1850 and the market hall built at a cost of £38,000.

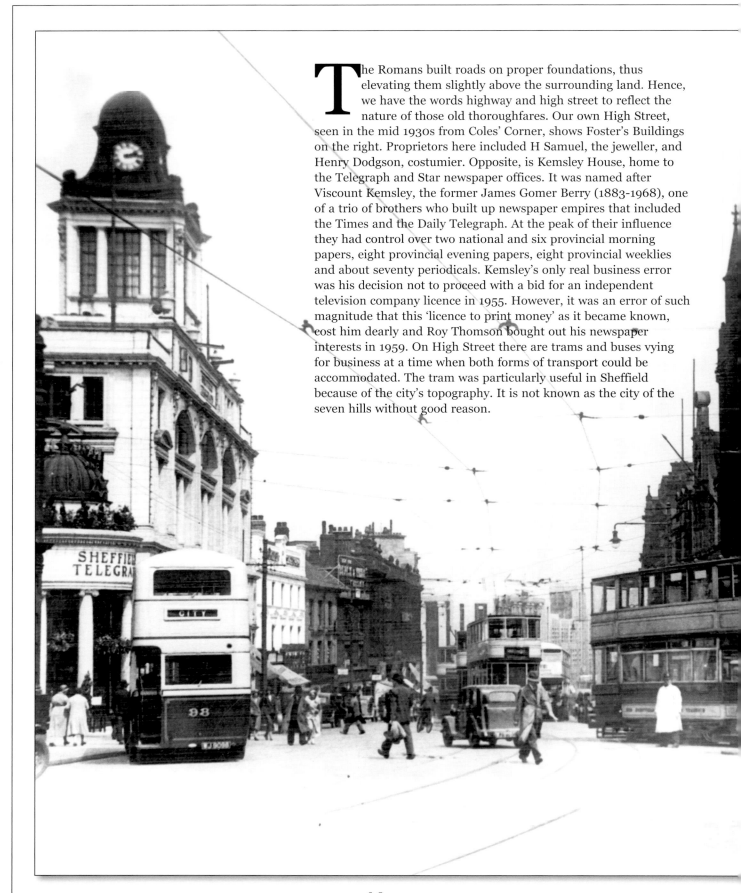

The Romans built roads on proper foundations, thus elevating them slightly above the surrounding land. Hence, we have the words highway and high street to reflect the nature of those old thoroughfares. Our own High Street, seen in the mid 1930s from Coles' Corner, shows Foster's Buildings on the right. Proprietors here included H Samuel, the jeweller, and Henry Dodgson, costumier. Opposite, is Kemsley House, home to the Telegraph and Star newspaper offices. It was named after Viscount Kemsley, the former James Gomer Berry (1883-1968), one of a trio of brothers who built up newspaper empires that included the Times and the Daily Telegraph. At the peak of their influence they had control over two national and six provincial morning papers, eight provincial evening papers, eight provincial weeklies and about seventy periodicals. Kemsley's only real business error was his decision not to proceed with a bid for an independent television company licence in 1955. However, it was an error of such magnitude that this 'licence to print money' as it became known, cost him dearly and Roy Thomson bought out his newspaper interests in 1959. On High Street there are trams and buses vying for business at a time when both forms of transport could be accommodated. The tram was particularly useful in Sheffield because of the city's topography. It is not known as the city of the seven hills without good reason.

Above: Quite what the caravan was doing on High Street in the mid 1950s is a mystery. Perhaps it had taken a wrong turning for Cleethorpes, but the bobby on point duty was happy to see it on its way, whatever the destination. Perched on his dais, looking a little like a white-coated budgie, this upholder of the law was a common sight in city centres as the increase in car ownership during that decade brought traffic-flow problems to a head for, perhaps, the first real time in our history. Thoroughfares built to allow horses and carts or the occasional stagecoach to pass through, could not cope with the increase in the volume of road users. Traffic lights and roundabouts, largely instituted in the 1930s, eased the problem for a while, but many crossroads and intersections needed assistance from the long arm of the law as everything ground to a halt. This scene was being played out in front of the Telegraph and Star offices. The history of these newspapers is a little confusing. The Star began life as the Sheffield Evening Telegraph in 1887, but by the following year was known as the Evening Telegraph and Star and Sheffield Daily Times. From 1898 it operated under the Yorkshire Telegraph and Star banner before becoming the Telegraph and Star in 1937 and just the Star the year later. This is now the city's daily paper and the Telegraph is published as a separate entity on a weekly basis.

Above: Firth Park is a 36 acre space given to the city by Alderman Mark Firth, an industrialist who was the town's mayor in 1874 and the Master Cutler 1867-69. This public benefactor donated the park that was originally part of the Page Hall estate in 1875 in an official ceremony overseen by the Prince of Wales, the future King Edward VII. This busy roundabout, not far from the park itself, was photographed in 1947 and also shows a branch of the Yorkshire Penny Bank. The 'penny' was dropped in 1959, on the occasion of the Bank's centenary. Climatically, 1947 was a memorable year. In February, heavy snowstorms and sub zero temperatures combined with a serious fuel shortage to bring Britain to its economic knees. Thousands of homes were without heat or light for long periods of the day. When the thaw came, many low lying districts were hit by floodwater, bringing further misery to a population that was still in the throes of wartime rationing. Many muttered about peacetime conditions being more uncomfortable than those experienced in the war, but the summer brought a marked change. It was one of the best on record and the country baked in long spells of glorious sunshine.

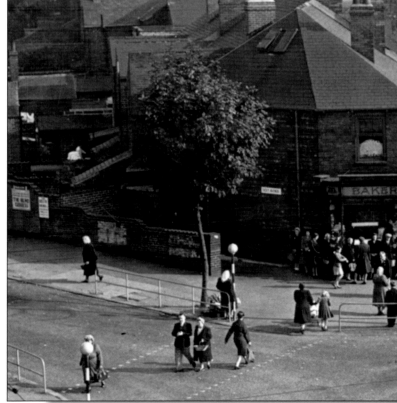

Below: An elevated view of Bellhouse Road, looking towards the Flower Estate with the National Provincial Bank, Wharncliffe Hotel and St Hilda's church in view, was captured during the late 1940s. But, what's in a name? This area was once called Pismire Hill, but the delicate sensibilities of residents in late Victorian times did not think much of the name of their locality. A long campaign to have it changed resulted in the council giving way in August 1902, much to the relief of one demure soul who always told friends and relatives that she lived at Primrose Hill. However, Bellhouse was chosen as the new name, after a group of cottages nearby.

The Flower Estate gets its name from its streets, which are named after flowers, and is an example of a garden suburb. Its design was influenced by people who had also worked on the famous garden suburbs of Bournville and Letchworth. The development began with the Yorkshire and North Midland Cottage Exhibition, held in 1907. Sheffield Corporation bought all the exhibition houses, though no further development took place for another five years. With the advent of World War I, further building was suspended and not completed until 1923. It was hit during the blitz in World War II, but, despite being restored to some of its former glory, later became quite run down.

Below: Pond Hill is off to the right as we look along Flat Street from Pond Street with Fitzalan Square in the distance. On the left, an advertising hoarding reminds us that 'Guinness is good for you'. The year is 1951 and television advertising had still to be invented. The first to be broadcast was one for Gibbs SR toothpaste in 1955, but many people missed it as the BBC attempted to steal ITV's thunder by killing off Grace Archer in a fire during an episode of its popular radio show, 'The Archers'. Before the advent of independent television, large scale advertising was therefore limited to newspapers, magazines and the cinema. It was backed up by the sort of poster we can see here and, to attract our attention, slogan writers of the 1950s came up with a variety of catchy lines. Rice Krispies had their snap, crackle and pop, while Rowntree's reminded us not to forget the fruit gums, mum (chum). Murraymints were too good to hurry and Fry's Turkish Delight had that eastern promise. However, locals on Flat Street had other things than beer, breakfast and sweeties to consider in 1951. A general election was called and the voters decided that they had had enough of Labour's attempts to get the country back on its feet and returned Winston Churchill to power.

Above: This elevated view of Sheaf Street from the junction with Broad Street shows the bustling Sheaf Market of the 1950s on the right. A series of wagons and trucks, plus parked cars and goods strewn across the pavement, add to the chaos of this scene. It must have been frustrating for the bus and tram drivers as they attempted to negotiate their vehicles past this hurly-burly. The market, commonly known as the 'Rag and Tag', was taken over by the Corporation from the Duke of Norfolk in 1899 and left it much as it was for many years. However, locals enjoyed its atmosphere, as well as the value for money, and many were not best pleased when a new indoor market replaced it in 1973. The adverts for Bass, Bisto, Gold Flake and the rest on the hoardings are evocative of the time when the odd slogan plus a picture of the product was sufficient to sell a product. There was no need for clever graphics or outlandish storylines behind a promotion; just a reliable product delivering what it aimed to was deemed to be sufficient. All this area is unrecognisable, now that the ring road has been developed. There is no place today for the horse and cart we can see on the left gently heading away from the camera.

This elevated view across Fitzalan Square and towards Commercial Street shows Barclays Bank and the News Theatre, on the right. They can be seen over the head of the statue of King Edward VII, a monument to the short reign (1901-10) of a loved monarch who made several visits to this city. A scheme to commemorate the late king appeared in February 1911 in the Sheffield Daily Telegraph and Alfred Drury (1857-1944) was commissioned to undertake the work. The statue was unveiled by the Duke of Norfolk on 27 October 1913. At that time, the News Theatre was only two years old and was known as the Electra Palace. Its elegant façade drew many an admiring glance because of its imaginative design. Inside, it was the last word in luxury with its artfully displayed floral arrangements, plush tip-up seating, electric lighting and stained glass windows. It re-equipped for sound in 1930 and underwent further change after World War II, becoming the News Theatre, concentrating on topical events. It further evolved into the Classic Cinema in the 1960s before closing in 1982. It was destroyed in a fire two years later. The new supertrams now whiz along here, reminding us that, in July 1905, Edward VII opened the electric tramway in Sheffield 11 years after the Corporation took control of the horse-drawn facility.

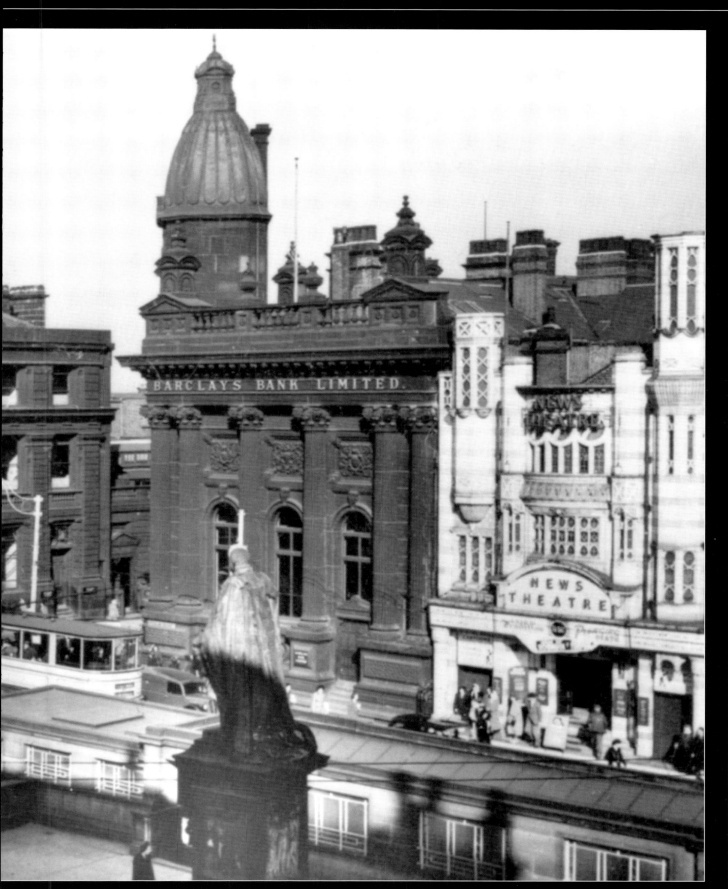

Below: Sheffield achieved city status in 1893, but it did not get its first bishop until 1914 as it was still part of the Diocese of York until it got its own identity when Leonard Hadley Burrows was appointed. He took up residence at Broomhill House, but did not like the place and sold it to the University in 1918. The cathedral church of Saints Peter and Paul on Church Street is mainly 15th century in architectural design, though it was restored in the late 1700s and again in 1880. There is evidence that the site was used for Christian worship as far back as the 9th century. Having been involved in alterations after the first world war, architect Charles Nicholson drew up plans for further changes and built a model of the proposal in the mid-1930s. However, with the coming of the war, these were shelved and, as there was so much rebuilding of bomb damaged property, they were never revived in peacetime. A more modest extension was overseen by Arthur Bailey in the 1960s, but this was during the decade following the date of this photograph. Habits have changed since then and the regular Sunday morning visit to the local parish church has become the exception rather than the rule.

Right: Taken from a dizzy height, the cameraman pointed his lens across Town Hall Square in the early 1950s. This was a decade when life styles changed dramatically, and none more so than in the home. A family car appeared on the driveway or on the street outside a house that was built at a time when car ownership for the man in the street was unthinkable. Inside the house, mum's day was made so much easier by the acquisition of a twin tub washing machine and electric iron. Gone were the washday red hands and aching backs spent over the mangle and dolly tub. Some homes even had fridges and housewives could make do with a weekly shop, knowing that perishables could last so much longer. The daily excursion to the shops became a thing of the past. In the evening, family entertainment switched from 'Journey into space' or 'The Archers' on the radio to shows that starred Peter Butterworth or Charlie Drake and even had American imports such as 'Amos 'n' Andy' or 'I Love Lucy'. The trams in the photograph were to undergo changes as they were phased out and completely disappeared as the next decade began. The golden age of the tramways lasted for about 30 years from the start of the last century, but took another 30 to die. The last city system in Britain ran in Glasgow, up to 1962. Although the Supertram, Metro and others, here and in other towns, have enjoyed recent success, those glorious days are gone forever.

Above right: Private car ownership increased dramatically in the 1950s, as we can see from this look along Church Street towards High Street. Once the preserve of the middle classes, motoring became affordable with the upturn in the economy and the fall in prices asked for family saloons. Such models as the Ford Popular, Morris Minor

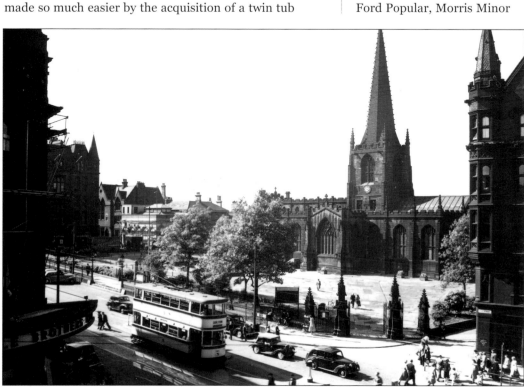

and Hillman Imp were snapped up by ordinary working class folk who had previously relied on public transport to

get them to work or out for a day at the weekend. A row of cars parked by the Anglican cathedral gave a warning, though, of the traffic problems that lay ahead because the city streets were not built to cope with the increased volume of traffic that was to come. Before long, there would be jams and gridlock as the centre ground to a halt. The cathedral site has had a church there since Saxon times. Rebuilt and modified over the centuries, it is steeped in history. It has always been a parish church and was consecrated as the Sheffield diocesan cathedral in 1914. At the end of World War I, plans were made to enlarge the building. These involved turning the axis of the church through 90 degrees, constructing a second tower and spire and building a new chancel and sanctuary on the north side of the old church, with the nave stretching out to Church Street on the south side. Church Lane, as it once was known, had been widened at the expense of the churchyard in 1785 and further developed in Victorian times.

Below: The swinging 60s brought changes to Britain, especially on the cultural and economic front. The country had cast off the drab days of the previous decade and was booming again. Attitudes towards the old values were beginning to shift, nowhere better seen than in the polling booths. A reactionary Tory government, headed up by a former peer in Alec Douglas Home, was sent packing. Young people began to demand a voice as they were no longer content with blind acceptance of what their elders and supposed betters told them to do. After all, they had money in their pockets and the economic wherewithal to influence society. Shops were turned into boutiques, dance halls became discos and barber's turned into unisex hairdressers. Women's hemlines went up, along with the blood pressure of their fathers, and young men began to wash their hair instead of slapping Brylcreem all over it. Looking along Flat Street towards Pond Street, a Morris Minor can be seen in the foreground. This rival to the Germans' people's car, the Volkswagen, was designed by Alec Issigonis, who was influential in the fortunes of Morris and BMC as he also later helped produce the top selling Mini. Both cars became cherished vehicles and inspired motorists' clubs.

Left: Commercial Street was named after the Commercial Inn that once stood at the head of Haymarket, facing down towards Waingate. This was a coaching inn sold at auction in 1866 for £3,950, making it the most expensive property in Sheffield at that time. As we look along Commercial Street and towards the Gas Company Offices from High Street, we can see the Yorkshire Bank on the left, on the corner of Haymarket, with Barclays Bank to the right on the edge of Fitzalan Square. This photograph from the 1960s shows a fairly quiet moment in what was normally a bustling scene. Perhaps it was coming towards the end of the day as Sheffield entered that period of hiatus between the end of office hours and the start of evening entertainment. However, the city was not exactly a thriving night scene in those days. The last bus left before 11 pm as they had to get to their outer termini and on to the sheds to be tucked up until morning. Anyone out and about at midnight had to have the wherewithal to afford an expensive taxi and, usually, the only hordes to be seen were not late night revellers but an army of street cleaners complete with brushes and pans.

Below: A man in his shirtsleeves was enjoying a pleasant spell of weather in 1959 as he sat on the wall by the railings that enclosed the gardens outside City Hall. Built of Darley Dale stone, the building opened on 22 September 1932 and continues to be an exciting entertainment and arts venue today. The gardens are also known as Balm Green Gardens and are situated on Barkers Pool, near where a pair of glass-cased modern fountains are now located. It was originally a place where drinking water was stored in the 15th century and, on occasion, water was channelled through the town from here to clean the streets, before issuing into the River Don. The pool, named after the man who built the old reservoir, came to be regarded as a nuisance and, in 1793, it was filled in. The Gaumont Cinema, on the right, later became the Odeon before being transformed into the Kingdom Nightclub. This is now one of the main talking points of anyone passing along here. For some, it is a modern building, but for others it is now a hideous, garish mishmash of glass and girders that would turn the Prince of Wales an apoplectic purple were he be asked to comment upon it. At least the Town Hall, seen towering above, provides the sort of attractive, conventional sight that most of us prefer.

ROYAL VISITS

Below: This royal visit to Sheffield was made in the 1920s long before the Duke of York would be thrust into the limelight as our king. Even in this photograph it is apparent that he was a man who was uncomfortable in having to take centre stage. Despite the warmth of the cheering crowds, his whole body language suggests someone who wishes he was somewhere else. The general public was very keen to get a glimpse of such an important dignitary. Modern generations have become satiated with moving images conveyed into their living rooms that strip bare every detail of someone's life, but these were the days when even talkies at the cinema had still not arrived. Other than newspaper photographs, just brief, silent newsreel footage in the picture house was the only way our forefathers could observe important figures. It is not surprising that a sea of faces greeted the duke's visit. Born Albert Frederick Arthur George in 1895, the second son of the future George V, 'Bertie' became the Duke of York in 1920. He married Elizabeth Bowes-Lyons in 1923. Little did the Sheffield public realise that it was witnessing a visit from the future king because, during a critical time for the monarchy in late 1936, the Duke's brother, Edward VIII, was to abdicate and force his brother to take on his mantle.

Right: During the war, many others might have scurried away to the West Indies, Canada or some remote corner of the globe, but not our king and queen. They endeared themselves to the nation by staying put. When Buckingham Palace suffered bomb damage, the Queen was heard to remark that she could now look eastenders in the face, referring to the battering that part of London took in the Blitz. Quite often, for obvious reasons of security, the royal couple's movements were kept secret. It would not have been sensible to advertise the fact that they were in a particular location at a certain time or Herr Goering's Luftwaffe or some sleeping subversive might have paid a call. So, when King George VI and Queen Elizabeth came to call on 6 January 1941, there were no crowds lining the streets as would have happened in peacetime. But, those who were able to see them were delighted that they had made the journey. The

was obviously moved by some of the harrowing tales she heard and the first hand experiences she gained and left commenting on the steadfast nature of northern folk.

Left: King George VI and Queen Elizabeth were in earnest conversation with both the dignitaries and the ordinary Sheffield people when they toured the war-damaged parts of the city in early 1941. She often took the lead and was always the guiding hand on the throne as her husband, though good hearted, was a poor communicator. He never properly controlled a stammer that became more obvious in stressful circumstances. Even in this photograph, his wife can be seen looking a little anxious for him as he chatted to those around him. George, or Bertie as he was known to his family, had not been prepared for such a public presence. He only came to throne in late 1936, following his brother's abdication. His wife never forgave the former king, Edward VIII, for exposing her husband to the rigours of the throne. Although it was lung cancer that killed him in 1952, she always felt that he became more susceptible to illness because of the stress to which he was subjected. Queen Elizabeth also reserved her greatest venom for Wallis Simpson, the American socialite whose involvement with Edward created the abdication crisis. Nor was she impressed with the former king's meetings with Hitler before the war as, once hostilities had broken out, there were rumours that the Germans would replace George with Edward on the British throne should the Nazis win the war. The idea of Queen Wallis was too much.

royals came to pay a special call on places that had suffered during the bombing raids that had reduced parts of Sheffield to rubble. Their thoughtfulness was much appreciated, knowing that they had not stayed in some ivory tower but had made a personal visit. The Queen

Below: Now, where has that Philip got to? Looking rather pensive, Queen Elizabeth, nevertheless, looked quite striking as she gazed across the square during her visit in the autumn of 1954. As always, a fashionable handbag nestled in the crook of her arm. This accessory has always been a must for Her Majesty and is one that has been adopted by other important ladies down the years. No picture of Margaret Thatcher, the queen of British politics in the 1980s, would be complete without her handbag. However, politicians come and go and their star eventually burns out. Monarchs last forever. Already our queen, now into her 80s, has notched up a reign that has outdone that of the vast majority of her predecessors. Only George III and Victoria will have outserved her by early 2008. Elizabeth came to throne in 1952, following the death of her father, George VI. As a youngster she was a happy child, not too interested in the airs and graces of court life. She was more at home being a member of a Brownie pack when, as a young 10 year old, she suddenly discovered that she was first in line to a throne that she never anticipated coming her way. Life had to change and the grooming for her future role began. Much of the moulding of the next monarch was given over to 'Crawfie', the seemingly faithful governess, Marion Crawford, who in 1950 published the story of her life with the royals and was completely ostracised for evermore.

Any open top motorcade that includes such a scene immediately brings back to mind that awful day in late 1963 when the president of the United States was gunned down. Those of us who witnessed the film footage can never forget the sight of John Kennedy being cradled by his wife, Jackie, as the life ebbed out of the charismatic leader. Our queen and her husband little realised that they were vulnerable targets as they waved to the thousands lining the streets when they paid an official visit in October 1954. Although security was an aspect of any planning related to their time in the city, the royal couple was so well loved that nobody imagined that harm could befall them. The duo represented the hopes of the public that a new dawn was heralded and that the birth of a second Elizabethan age had been witnessed. The country was just coming out of the austerity of the immediate postwar period and the future was bright, or so we wanted to believe. Queen Elizabeth had been our monarch for less than three years, but she already knew how to win the hearts and minds of her subjects with that radiant smile. Even the sun shone brightly as office workers hung precariously from windows and children, granted the day off school, cheered wildly and waved little flags as the Rolls Royce and its passengers motored along High Street.

WARTIME

Who do you think you are kidding, Mr Hitler? The boys from the Home Guard, seen here being inspected by Lt General Sir Ronald Adams on Blonk Street, a road named after a scissorsmith, started off as a laughing stock. Known originally as the Local Defence Volunteers (LDV), they often paraded with broom handles masquerading as rifles and trained for grenade throwing practice using tennis balls. General Walter Kirke founded the force in February 1940. Initially devised as a means to defend the critical port of Dover, the ranks swelled quickly with local volunteers, too old to enlist but eager to fight. Several months later, Winston Churchill suggested renaming the LDV as the Home Guard. By then, there were over a million members, all keen to help the nation in its hour of need. Although not properly armed until 1943, the volunteers performed noble work manning coastal defences and anti aircraft guns, firewatching and defensive manoeuvres designed to thwart attacks by paratroopers. They manned guard posts and performed other duties to free up regular troops for service overseas. As the threat of invasion had long passed, the Home Guard was stood down in December 1944 and formally disbanded a year later. A modernised version of the Home Guard was briefly re-established in December 1951. Although units in coastal areas were authorised to recruit to full strength, it fell foul of a complete reassessment of Britain's defence position following the advent of the H bomb and was disbanded in July 1957.

Below: Even the rescue teams from the civil defence organisations were stunned by the carnage around Fitzalan Square. In their heart of hearts, they knew it was on the cards, but nothing prepared them for the stark reality of the destruction wreaked by the German bombers that struck during the night of 12-13 December 1940. Sheffield manufactured munitions, armour plate and aircraft parts for the military and was a strategic target for the enemy. After the failure of its fighter planes' attempt to subdue us in the late summer of 1940, during the Battle of Britain, the Luftwaffe embarked on its systematic bombing of ports and industrial centres. Glasgow, Manchester, London, Liverpool and Exeter were just some of the cities that received a series of visits that left a trail of death and destruction behind. The night that Sheffield will never forget was cloudier than attacking planes liked. They preferred perfect vision and a full moon, but low cloud hung over the city. The first wave dropped incendiaries to mark the path for the following planes to dump their loads of high explosive on selected targets below. However, because of the visibility fires were started close to the city centre and not near the factories along the Don valley as intended. People knew what was coming and rushed to take what shelter they could, but death and destruction were inevitable once the bombs started falling.

Above: The civil defence did its best in clearing up after the air raids of 12-13 December 1940, but it was a mammoth task. When the main attack got under way, buildings around Campo Lane and Vicar Lane were flattened, but the most dramatic destruction took place around High Street when the C&A store was blasted by a 1,000 lb bomb. Across the way, the Marples Hotel and neighbouring buildings also suffered extensive damage. Many had taken refuge in the Marples as it had extensive cellars that they presumed would act as a protective air raid shelter. The hotel then took a direct hit an hour after the first strike. A bomb came straight through the roof and detonated at ground floor level, right above the place where frightened staff, guests and members of the public had taken refuge. It was never known exactly how many died on that spot, as most could only be identified from their personal effects. Some of the victims were literally blown apart. Somehow, seven men escaped serious injury, but about 70 were killed and that included a number who were never properly identified. Joe Davis, the world billiards and snooker champion was a fortunate man. He was booked to play an exhibition match there that evening, but could not get there as the railway line from Hull had been bombed. In all, Sheffield lost over 600 souls to different air raids across the city.

Below: Barrage balloons were tethered to the ground with metal cables and used as a defence against enemy bombardment by damaging the aircraft on collision with the cables. Some versions carried small explosive charges that would be pulled up against a plane to ensure its destruction. They were only regularly employed against low-flying aircraft, the weight of a longer cable making them impractical for higher altitudes. These women, playing an active part in the nation's defences against the Nazis, were enjoying a refreshment break on Petre Street, named after Lord Petre, one of the trustees of the Duke of Norfolk's estate to whom he was related by marriage. The British Balloon Command was established in 1938 when, despite Mr Chamberlain's naive belief in Herr Hitler's assurances that he had few territorial ambitions, many in the military knew that war was inevitable. Dive bombers had been used effectively in the Spanish Civil War, notably on Guernica, the picturesque Basque town obliterated by German planes. Barrage balloons provided the sort of cover that this form of attack would find difficult to penetrate. A club for those who served in barrage balloon squadrons was established after the war and, perhaps, these gallant girls of the Women's Auxiliary Air Force were able to swap tales and share memories of their part in the conflict for many years to come.

Right: Although the cost of the war included millions of lives, there was also the added financial burden on the country as daily life was disrupted and valuable resources deployed in repairing bomb damage. Fitzalan Square was just one of the city centre locations badly damaged in the air raids of late 1940. Here, tram tracks were torn apart

and, beyond the twisted metal, we can see some of the damage inflicted upon nearby buildings. There were many glum expressions on the faces of the men who had a mammoth repair task in front of them. The alert sounded 130 times during the war and, although most of them were false alarms due to enemy aircraft flying across the region while on their way to other targets, on 16 occasions the sirens were genuine calls to the air raid shelters. In Sheffield, precautions against air raids were in hand before a declaration of war with Germany had been made on 3 September 1939. Anderson shelters, made out of corrugated steel, were being delivered to many householders and city centre buildings were soon sandbagged and their windows taped once the Nazis moved into Poland. The first flights across the city were mainly reconnaissance missions by the Luftwaffe but, on the night of 18 August 1940, the first bomb fell for real and acted as a warning for the blitz that came four months later.

Above right: In 1942, when these women war workers at the English Steel Corporation were photographed, the country relied heavily on the fairer sex to keep industry going. With so many men at the front, it was essential that production continued at an even quicker rate than in peacetime. Women joined the land army, drove buses and entered the armed

forces as support workers. However, just as in the first world war, many opted for factory work as the way that they could do their bit. They worked in all manner of production ranging from making ammunition to uniforms and aeroplanes. The hours they worked were long and some women had to move to where the factories were, consequently being paid more. Skilled women could earn £2.15s a week and to them this must have seemed a lot, but men doing the same work were paid more. In fact, it was not unknown for unskilled men to get more money than skilled female workers. This inequality caused Glaswegians in a Rolls Royce factory to go on strike, even though there was a war on. Despite some ill feeling about wages, these Sheffield workers looked happy enough. Many friendships formed at the workplace lasted a lifetime and gave the workers plenty to reminisce about when they returned to the kitchen sink when their men returned from the front. However, there were large numbers who resented having to go back to household drudgery.

Below: Oh how we celebrated on Victory in Europe (VE) Day. Colwall Street, Attercliffe was no different from thousands of other similar streets all over Britain. The whole country erupted with a mixture of joy and relief. After nearly six years of fighting the Germans, it was all over. The desperate days of drabness, shortages, blitzes, death and despair were temporarily forgotten in the blaze of multi-coloured flags, fireworks and floodlights. Civilians linked arms with servicemen and whooped at the tops of their voices. Complete strangers hugged and kissed each other. Huge congas and hokey-cokeys were danced around the statues in the city centre. Trestle tables were dragged out of church halls and schoolrooms and set out in the back streets as neighbours mucked in together for impromptu street parties. A week's ration was blown in just one afternoon. But, what the heck? We had something worth celebrating and somehow little buns, sandwiches and jugs of lemonade appeared. Children made party hats from bits of paper and card that had escaped the salvage drives. An old wind up gramophone was requisitioned. We had not partied since the Coronation in 1937. Everyone was happy for this day, the like of which would never be seen again, though Victory in Japan (VJ) Day ran it close three months later when the war in the Far East ended.

Above: As a venue for a Victory in Europe (VE) Day celebration, Dunkirk Square was aptly named in that it brought back to mind one of the low spots, but at the same time successes, of World War II. In 1940, British troops suffered the humiliation of being driven out of France by the might of the German military. Our troops were forced back to the beaches at Dunkirk in northern France with little hope of salvation. Then came one of the most remarkable rescue missions of all time. Initially, the Royal Navy mounted an evacuation exercise, but soon realised that it had insufficient ships to cope with the massive numbers awaiting rescue. The call went out along the south coast for help from any sort of boat that could lend a hand. A flotilla of smacks, launches, fishing boats and pleasure craft swarmed across the Channel. Somehow, despite the strafing from enemy aircraft, thousands of soldiers were brought home to fight another day. Many brave part-time sailors and fishermen gave their lives in the mission and, although everyone celebrated VE Day in May 1945 with street parties and cheerful celebrations, there was a touch of sadness when we recalled those who would not be coming back to share in the fun. Some of the mothers in their pinnies would have no husbands to welcome back to Dunkirk Square.

Ways of bolstering morale among the population were always being sought during the early days of the second world war. After the initial quiet for the first few months of the phoney war that followed the declaration of hostilities in 1939, major setbacks abroad in Norway and the evacuation from Dunkirk, allied with the bombing raids on our towns, the public knew that it was in for a grim struggle. The government took every propaganda opportunity it could to lift our spirits. The Battle of Britain in the late summer and early autumn of 1940 provided such a chance. At last we had some success to celebrate and, as a backdrop to the Sheffield Newspapers' War Fund drive, an enemy plane was paraded for all to see on the Albert Hall site at Barkers

Pool. Shot down over Margate in September, this Messerschmitt 109 was one of the fighter planes with which our brave boys in blue did battle in the skies over the south coast and the home counties. Prime Minister Churchill was moved to make his famous 'never in the field of human conflict was so much owed by so many to so few' speech in Parliament. The Me109 was one of the fastest fighter planes around and over 35,000 were built for the Luftwaffe during the war. Thankfully, we had able pilots and our own tiptop aircraft, the aptly named Spitfire. Hurricanes were also out in force during the Battle of Britain, but they tended to focus on enemy bombers. It was the Supermarine Spitfire, designed by RJ Mitchell, that took on the likes of the ME Bf-109 and sent it packing.

Swann-Morton - The Leading Edge

Sheffield's Swann-Morton Company manufactures more than a million surgical and craft blades every single day. Celebrating 75 years of being in business in 2007, the firm is justly proud of its remarkable achievements.

It was in August 1932, with a capital of just £150, that the firm began making and selling a range of razor blades. Even before they began business the firm's founders drew up four statements to guide them in the ethical

Above: Company founders Mr W R Swann and Miss Doris Fairweather. Right: Swann Morton's first premises in 1932. Below: The second factory founded in 1935 on Bradfield Road, Sheffield.

consequences of their entry into the world of commerce. The statements were written out on the firm's headed notepaper in Walter R Swann's own handwriting, one copy of which has survived the ensuing years.

In 1917, after leaving grammar school, Walter Swann became an apprentice engineer. He also became a convinced socialist. In 1924 he found himself working with Miss Doris Fairweather, a supervisor in charge of a group of women making razor blades.

It was in 1925 that Mr.Swann, apparently close to being sacked for his trade union activities, accepted a position establishing a razor blade department in another firm. Doris Fairweather, together with a number of women in her charge and another fitter, followed Swann.

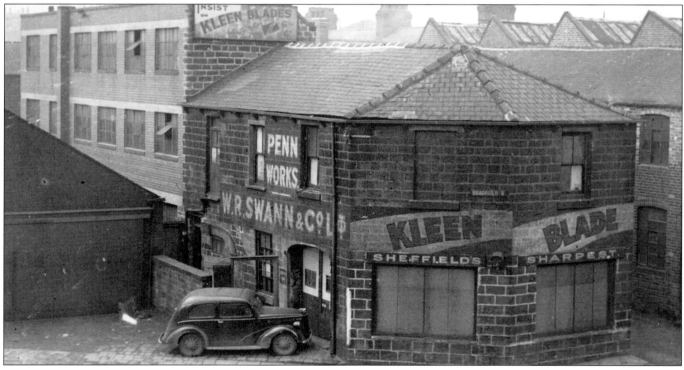

In 1932, just six years later, Mr.Swann left to found his own firm, W R Swann & Co Ltd. along with metallurgist J Alfred Morton. Doris Fairweather and her team followed. The fledgling firm began in a workshop behind houses in Sheffield's Woodlands Street. Miss Fairweather, as she was always known, was a strong disciplinarian, a trait inherited from her father who had been a regimental sergeant major.

Building their own machinery they developed new devices, kept quality and service at a very high level and put all profits back into growth. By 1935 they were soundly based and made a move to marginally better premises in Bradfield Road. Around this time the firm was approached by a surgical supplier to make replaceable blades for scalpels with a patented design of handle. Sales for the handle however did not come up to expectations and the work came to an end. The firm had however discovered that the American patent for the handle had run out. So it was decided not to allow Swann-Morton's new know-how to be wasted. Accordingly the firm made tools and the Swann-Morton scalpel was born. Today it boasts 90 per cent of the British trade in such products, with exports to over 100 countries.

From then until the outbreak of war in 1939 there was rapid growth. Each Christmas substantial cash presents were given to its workers: in those days an unusual gesture.

A 40 hour working week was introduced, an innovation which was soon followed with rather greater publicity by Boots of Nottingham. All holidays were paid for.

In 1938 the growing firm bought the first piece of land for the erection of part of the present factory, the Penn works at Owlerton Green. The first four workshops were completed in 1939 just as the war started. Surgical knives were required in ever-greater quantities- and as the company's efficiency increased it was able to reduce prices, the directors not wishing to make a profit out of the war. That policy turned out to be a mistake: customers thought that the quality couldn't be good enough at such a low price!

Top: The growing factory in 1939. Left: Making razor blades in the early years.

Ironically, given the firm's founding principles, the application of socialism elsewhere caused it great problems after the war. With a Labour government elected at the war's end taxation was increased to ominous proportions. Even so the company still went forward with its growth policy and a second stage of building took place at Owlerton Green producing the administration and office block as well as flats for Walter Swann and a caretaker. By then the firm had a work force of approximately 100.

Alfred Morton left the company in the post war period leaving Walter Swann and Doris Fairweather as the two remaining co-directors.

Concerned over unemployment in Scotland the pair thought they would do well to start a factory there for razor blade making. This would prove to be a mistake: an example of sentimentality overriding sound commercial judgment.

After seven months working in Scotland they had to close down the Scottish factory and prune the Sheffield base, getting down to a period of austere working to pay their taxes. Politics, economics, finance: they knew something about the first two but little about the third. They learned the hard way and eventually came up smiling. Before then however Purchase Tax had been applied to razor blades, and the last straw came when the firm had to pay tax on a million razor blades given away free as samples.

In the 1950s the company decided to steadily run down the making of razor blades, having had enough taxation, and set about concentrating on untaxed scalpels and fine industrial edges.

During the ten years from 1947 to 1957, despite its tax troubles, the firm went on with its third stage of building, putting everything back into plant and buildings with the exception of the few thousand pounds paid out to workers at Christmas time.

Sales were increasing, production growing, and technical efficiency and research improving all the time to produce ever-increasing profits. By 1957 the firm was manufacturing 38 million blades each year, 100,000 each working day and using 140 tons of Sheffield-made strip steel. A superannuation scheme was started in 1957, at first limited to the key people within the organisation. Two directors and a secretary had died as well as others including the first fitter who had been with the firm from the outset; the result being their widows were reasonably well provided for.

Top: The works canteen in the 1940s. Mr Swann leaning and Miss Fairweather, right.
Above: An early view inside the Grinding Department.

Now in a sideways move Walter Swann decided to invest in food production, creating a profitable orchard which could cheaply supply at least part of the workforce's food. By 1961 S M (Growers) had come into being with orchard land and properties in the Wisbech area of Cambridgeshire. Packing buildings and cold storage chambers were built to the same high standard that characterised the Sheffield factory. Many thousands of young trees were planted and everything was done to lay the foundations for modern fruit growing in a competitive world.

Back in Sheffield by 1964 the fourth stage of building took place giving still more production capacity. Soon after that a demand for sterilised surgical blades began to arise. As the firm had been the prime movers in the use of Vapour Phase Inhibitor - VPI - paper inserted into foil to keep blades clean, dry and non-rusting, the firm got in touch with UKAE at Wantage, and with its co-operation developed the sterilisation of blades through gamma radiation.

It became clear that a cobalt plant on the premises would soon become a necessity as a part of the production line. In late 1964 a batch cobalt plant, the first of its kind in the world, was erected in premises built for that purpose. Visitors from many countries visited the works solely to see the new plant. Soon after being installed the throughput was such that further cobalt had to be loaded to cut down the sterilisation time in order to keep pace with growing demand. Meanwhile, in keeping with their founding principles, the directors felt that, whilst imaginative technical and administrative and commercial staff were essential to keep up the good works, they neither needed nor wanted shareholders outside the business. Indeed until a trustees' company was formed no dividends were ever paid.

As the wealth had been created, first out of the shaving public, then out of sick people, the directors continued to believe that the wealth created should not be for a few people to consume but to be used first in the interests of those who made it, and then in the medical world.

In the mid 1960s a trust was formed to administer the company in which the employees had a 50 per cent share, the other 50 per cent vested in a charitable holding. Walter Swann died in October 1980 and his co-director, Doris Fairweather died in February 1984 but their foresight in the 1960s ensured that this unique arrangement has seen the company go from strength to strength.

Left: *Inspection of blade fitment.*
Above: *An early Swann-Morton Surgeons Case.*
Below: *The factory taking shape in the 1950s.*

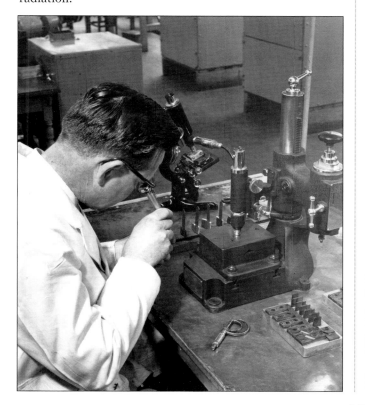

Achieving today's quality standards and complying with a multitude of complex rules and regulations may prove difficult for some companies, but for Swann-Morton it has just been a natural progression.

Operating a policy of self-design and build wherever possible gives the company a high degree of control over its production processes - and ideas for improvement from the factory floor are positively encouraged. The introduction of new technology has consistently put the company at the leading edge of surgical blade manufacture.

The installation of its own irradiation plant in the 1960s gave Swann-Morton complete self-sufficiency in product sterilization, and since the introduction in the late eighties of a state of the art irradiation centre complete with micro-biological laboratory it is also able to offer these facilities to other health-care manufacturers.

Quality control has always been of utmost importance with inspections taking place throughout the production processes. Indeed surgical blades are subject to two final inspections immediately prior to packaging the blade within a 'clean room' environment, after which blades are

sterilised in the on-site gamma irradiation facility, a service performed by the subsidiary company Swann-Morton (Services) Ltd. Such separation ensures total independence and control over all processes.

To complete the comprehensive facilities the microbiological laboratory provides an expert service for monitoring and identifying microbiological contamination, both environmental and product-borne, ensuring the highest possible standards.

At the turn of the new century Swann-Morton embarked on an extensive expansion programme involving major

Right: The increasingly hi-tech world of the Furnace Shop in 2000. Below: Part of the major expansion to the Packing Department.

Wherever a versatile, precision cutting blade is needed on every continent one will find a Swann-Morton product near at hand.

Today the company employs around 350 people and uses 600 tonnes of steel each year to make around 1.5 million surgical and craft blades daily. They are sold in virtually every country in the world. Almost two thirds of production is exported with a turnover exceeding £17 million a year. Yet Swann-Morton's founding principles still apply. The firm still has an extraordinary low turnover of employees who enjoy unique working conditions that include ten weeks holiday a year, a thirty-five hour week, double time for overtime, profit-related pay, private health care and a contributory pension scheme. There can be few businesses founded on a Utopian dream that have lasted beyond the lifetime of their founders, or which have continued to follow their original values despite becoming major undertakings.

Walter Swann and Doris Fairweather's legacy provides an extraordinary testimonial to their values - and a continuing example to others of what can be achieved through applying genuine moral principles in business. Those principles continue to help make Swann-Morton the triumph it is today. The desire for ongoing improvement, the hard work ethic of its employees and a policy of promotion from within sustain it as a world leader and will undoubtedly ensure that Swann-Morton remains at the leading edge throughout its next 75 years in business.

construction works. The investment of five and a half million pounds underlined Swann-Morton's confidence in the future.

In the 21st century that confidence in the future has led the company to invest in advanced tooling and press equipment which has in turn led to an intense machine building programme, particularly within the grinding and packing departments, with a resultant increase in output. The investment in new technology has also included an environmentally friendly state-of-the-art cleaning plant which recycles vapour from cleaning agents.

In 2006 a new facility was completed across the road from the Penn Works – in keeping with the 'Swan' theme called the Cobb Works. The two-storey building would house Swann-Morton's engineering and machine development sections along with additional warehousing. Space released within the main facility would help expand production capacity.

Whilst new opportunities within the western world still present themselves, especially in the USA, Swann-Morton also invests time and expertise in developing markets which are still emerging from years of economic and social depression.

Swann-Morton blades are used in the most demanding environment of all - the operating theatre. Continual development in response to customer demand has led to the creation of over sixty surgical blades and more than twenty handles. As surgical techniques have become ever more sophisticated Swann-Morton has risen to the challenges posed.

But the company's surgical blades are not only used in operating theatres; they are also the choice of dentists, chiropodists and veterinary surgeons and a host of professionals in industry, crafts and art studios.

Above: The new Reception area.
Below: An aerial view of Swann-Morton, 2007.

AT LEISURE

Above: Hucklow Road School was getting ready to celebrate Empire Day in 1948 with, among things, a display of country dancing. Dancing around a maypole, Cumberland reels, Oxo square dances and jolly jigs have rather disappeared from our lives. Celebrating Empire Day, as these girls were doing, must have seemed incongruous to many observers at the time. Britain went into the 1939-45 war as one of the superpowers with an empire stretching across the globe. The world map was covered in red. Yet, despite winning the conflict, we came out at the other end as a bankrupt nation, playing second fiddle to America and the USSR. Our empire began to crumble as India was partitioned into the two independent states of India and Pakistan. Burma and Ceylon quickly followed suit and gained autonomy. Our influence in Asia diminished and soon African countries began to flex their muscles.

Above: It was only in 1918 that compulsory education for children up to the age of 14 came onto the statute book. Quite often, though, youngsters went to an all age school, with only the more gifted or more wealthy attending a separate school that would give them a more specialised education that might lead on to higher things. Wadsley Bridge Council School, Penistone Road North, was typical of the sort of educational establishment that catered for our youngsters after the second world war. The 1944 Butler Education Act set up the tripartite system with which readers will be familiar, clearly defining the divide between primary and secondary schools. This group of primary age children, still segregated by gender for some activities, underwent a Physical Training session. It would not become known as Physical Education until later. The school leaving age was raised to 15 in 1947 and these lads largely grumbled about the extra year in school. However, they did have the chance to get to a grammar school via the 11 plus exam, a combination of arithmetic, English and IQ tests that offered the opportunity to gain a pathway to an academic education and a route to college or university. Those who failed the exam went to secondary modern or technical schools where the emphasis was on preparing for life as a member of the working classes.

Below: Handsworth has a number of reasons to be proud of its heritage as it is even mentioned in the Domesday Book. Benjamin Huntsman, one of the steel manufacturing pioneers, lived here in the 1740s, and William Jeffcock, who was born here in 1800, later became Sheffield's first Lord Mayor. Tradition counts for a lot in Handsworth and its sword dancing ritual has been practised for centuries. Using long steel swords, a team of eight men perform a dance which lasts just under 10 minutes and ends with all the swords being interlocked and held aloft by one man. Traditional music is played and the dancers wear a military style uniform. In 1953, these youngsters were watching some entertainment, perhaps provided by clowns who used to accompany the sword dancers, as they took part in the pageant to celebrate the coronation of Queen Elizabeth II. They look to have been lucky with the weather, because in London it was a dreary, damp day. The crowds lining the way to Westminster Abbey were drenched, though many were cheered by the sight of the Queen Salote of Tonga. This huge woman, soaked to the skin, rode in an open topped carriage that was rapidly filling with rainwater, yet beamed magnificently all the way along. These Handsworth children will be grandparents by now, but they will still recall this coronation day as there has not been another since.

Cinema going was one of the main sources of entertainment in the 1950s and picture houses flourished in the immediate postwar period. Taking in a flick was also part of the courting routine for any young couple who nervously held hands on a first date or cuddled up on the back row when going steady. Walking out with a young man, as our parents termed it, was one of the first steps towards that ring on the finger to which all girls aspired. With dad on the prowl if we were late home there was little chance of a goodnight kiss on the doorstep, so the dark of the cinema was a welcome escape from prying eyes.

By the late 1950s of this photograph, cinemas were coming under pressure from the boom in television and audiences started to fall off. The Wicker Picture House was one of those to feel the pinch. It was built at the start of World War I, but immediately pressed into service as a steelworks' warehouse. It opened as a cinema on 14 June 1920, showing DW Griffith's 'Broken Blossoms', starring Lillian Gish. Sound reached the Wicker in 1930 when Al Jolson was the lead in 'The Jazz Singer'. It was renamed Studio 7 in 1962. It closed on 14 December 1982 but, despite a brief revival in 1986, finally shut down in 1987.

Below: Sheffield Picture Palace, or the Palace as it later became known, was the city's first purpose built cinema. Situated on Union Street, it admitted its first paying customers on 1 August 1910. Quite remarkably, it was managed by Leonard Shaw for 54 years in what must surely be a record that cannot or can never be matched. This delightfully designed building was the brainchild of Benton and Roberts, a local firm with offices on Surrey Street. The actual building work was carried out by George Longden and Son. Although primarily a picture house, it also had a stage and dressing rooms and could double as a theatre. At the time of its construction, going to the pictures was a novel pastime that not everyone thought would last. Hence, the financial backers hedged their bets. But, they need not have worried. The 1,000 seater auditorium was regularly filled, thanks to the success of such early silent movie glamour girls as Theda Bara, Lillian Gish and Mary Pickford. Men swooned over their beauty and women marvelled at their seductive ways, wondering why the blokes sitting next to them were no Douglas Fairbanks. All the while, the action on the screen was accompanied by musicians who set the mood with their apt choice of atmospheric playing. The Palace closed on 31 October 1964 with a showing of 'The King and I', starring Yul Brynner and Deborah Kerr. This was an odd choice, considering that the film was eight years old. The cinema has long been demolished.

Right: The Gaumont on Barkers Pool was a popular cinema with the Sheffield public and is seen on the evening of its gala opening as a two screen movie house in 1969 when the Rank organisation decided to try and bolster falling attendances with a choice of films. A third screen was added in 1979, but it rather lost its way and never recovered its former glory and closed on 7 November 1985. It gained its name in 1946, having opened on Boxing Day 1926 as the Regent. Designed by WE Trent, it was one of the grandest cinemas in the city. It boasted a large sculptured chimneypiece, terracotta vases, splendid mirrors and cut glass candelabras. The lounge was sumptuously and magnificently decorated and the walls adorned with paintings that suggested a moonlit Italian garden. At this reopening of the refurbished Gaumont, two very successful films were screened as a carrot to attract the public. 'Ice Station Zebra' is one of those adventure movies that still pops up on our television screens from time to time, 40 years after it was released. Starring Rock Hudson and Patrick McGoohan, it was based on the Alistair MacLean novel that told of American and Soviet secret agents trying to recover a lost capsule in the icy wastes of the North Pole. 'Funny Girl', with Barbra Streisand and Omar Sharif, was the story of Fanny Brice, a Broadway star. Streisand's performance won her an Oscar.

Right: In 1867, members of the Wednesday Cricket Club met at the Adelphi, a public house on the site of the present Crucible Theatre. A football team was formed, primarily as a fitness programme for the cricketers in the winter months. The club became a professional outfit in 1887 and was elevated to the Football League in 1892. The FA Cup was won in 1896 and again in 1907, both victories taking place at Crystal Palace. After World War I, the First Division title was won on two occasions and, in 1935, Sheffield Wednesday defeated West Bromwich Albion to lift the FA Cup in the highest scoring final that Wembley had seen. It was a goals tally that would not be beaten until Blackpool overcame Bolton Wanderers in a seven goal thriller in 1953. The Owls twice took the lead, only to be pegged back by a dogged Baggies' side, but two late strikes by winger Ellis Rimmer secured a 4-2 victory. Here, skipper Ronald Starling proudly carries the cup that his

colleagues had battled for so manfully. Ronnie played for Hull and Newcastle before signing for Wednesday in 1932 and won his first England cap in the following year. He was transferred to Aston Villa in 1937 and, after a spell as a coach with Nottingham Forest, ran a newsagent's not far from Hillsborough. He died in 1991, aged 81, the very year that the Owls won the League Cup Final at Wembley.

Below left: Owlerton Stadium was built in 1929, primarily for the burgeoning sport of speedway. Greyhound racing was introduced three years later and both pastimes have continued to attract a significant following ever since. Stock car racing and the occasional monster truck event are also featured. By the time this photograph was taken in the 1960s, Sheffield Tigers had covered many thousands of circuits of the cinder track. The noise from the exhausts and the smell of the burning rubber and warm ashes is something special to this sport.

Spectators on each bend duck for cover as the riders and machines jockey for position in what is a great night out for old and young alike. The site was formerly a village green where Buffalo Bill's circus once performed and his stirring daredevil show with bareback rider Red Indians, sharpshooters and lasso twirlers would have been just as exciting as watching Ron Bagley and Billy Bales race around the circuit. The stadium is probably named after the alder trees or 'owlers' that once grew here. It became part of the A & S Leisure Group in 1991 and has since undergone a £3 million improvement programme. Modern restaurants and corporate hospitality are now complementary to the day to day expectations of sports and betting fans.

Below: Remember the days when soccer was played on mud heaps, bumpy pitches and worn surfaces? The modern footballer cannot seem to manage unless the grass is cut in a particular way and is almost manicured to perfection. It is just as well that the pampered superstar of the 21st century does not have to cope with the conditions that Tony Currie, Joe Shaw or Jimmy Hagen experienced or he would not have been able to leave the safety of his air conditioned, automatic, cost a bomb Ferrari. This scene is from a match against the then high flying Leeds United on 24 April 1965 when Don Revie's team came to Bramall Lane to take on our own United. The visitors went away with a winning two points, as it was in those days, and the Blades continued to struggle until the end of the season, just avoiding relegation. The old cricket pavilion can be seen and is a reminder that county cricket was still played here at the time and would be for a further eight years. Sheffield United was formed in 1889 and soon recorded a score that remains a record today. During that first season it had the misfortune to be drawn against a crack Bolton Wanderers in the FA Cup. The 13-0 defeat acts as a reminder to Dave Bassett, Neil Warnock and others that things actually can get worse. The club was one of the founder members of the modern Premier League in 1992.

Above: The Library Theatre, Tudor Place, was originally used as a lecture hall and was built inside an existing building alongside the Lyceum Theatre. It was used as an air raid shelter during the second world war, but in 1947 dressing rooms were created and the hall became a legitimate theatre. However, with its small stage and restricted viewing, it struggled to satisfy both a dramatic need and full audience satisfaction. In 1961, some major remodelling of the interior was undertaken. The auditorium was raked, a proscenium arch added, the stage enlarged and the foyer improved. The theatre could now give 260 people an enjoyable and comfortable experience. This poster was advertising some of the varied events on offer in 1968. There was to be a recital of classical music and film shows, the latter including the hardly inspiring 'I walk around Moscow' and the 1942 'Ivan the Terrible', an aptly named movie that was rather heavy going. But, to be fair, if you wanted popular cinema then you went to one of the main picture houses. The Library Theatre looked to attract a more avant garde audience by offering specialist or offbeat fare to its customers. Sheffield does quite well for theatres with this one, the Lyceum, the Crucible and the Montgomery all enjoying success.

Below: Second only in soap opera longevity to 'The Archers', Granada TV's 'Coronation Street' has been entertaining us since 1960. Many of the characters became household names and quite a few actors moved on from the serial to bigger and better things in television and on the silver screen. Ben Kingsley, Arthur Lowe and Sarah Lancashire are just a few of those who graced the cobbled streets of the set. Some big names have enjoyed cameo appearances in Weatherfield, with Ian McKellen and Honor Blackman being notable recent examples. 'Corrie', as it is affectionately known, was still in its relative infancy when one of its early stars came to the Central Cinema on High Street, Beighton. Fans turned out in droves to see Pat Phoenix who played the role of the blousy Elsie Tanner. She was to be part of the cast for over 23 years before being written out of the show. She was born Patricia Pilkington in Manchester in 1924 and, in the 1940s and 1950s, toured the north of England in repertory theatre before getting her big break. She married three times, the last time just before her death in 1986 when she tied the knot with actor Tony Booth, thus becoming the mother in law of Cherie Blair, the wife of the future prime minister. Central Cinema opened in August 1913 and was rebuilt after a fire on 29 March 1922. It reopened in September 1923, but finally closed its doors 40 years later.

TRANSPORT

Two policemen were working in tandem on point duty in 1950, keeping the traffic flowing on High Street at Cole's Corner. A family with two young girls, smartly dressed with their little white bobbysox, waited at the central reservation for a tram to trundle by. No young female dressed in jeans or trousers in those days, nor did their parents, for that matter, if they were going to be out and about in the city. Cole's Corner was a well known meeting place as everyone knew exactly where it was. The department store was the first of its type in Sheffield when established by John Cole in 1869. It later became part of the Selfridge chain before being sold to John Lewis. Cole's relocated to Barkers Pool in 1963 and lost its original name. The old department store site was taken over by the Midland Bank and then the HSBC. A blue plaque was placed on the spot by the rotary Club to ensure that the memory of this famous shop is perpetuated. Somewhat quaintly, Sheffield born singer-songwriter Richard Hawley, a member of the Britpop scene of the 1990s in the group The Longpigs, has helped to bring Cole's Corner to the attention of the younger generation. In 2005 he released a single with that title and the album of the same name was nominated for a Mercury Music prize.

Right: The Hope and Anchor brewery, by then owned by Bass, bottled its last beer in 1993. There was a time when the cricket ground at Bramall Lane had a brewery at each end. It is said that the smell on match days inspired the Yorkshire team to greatness; they did after all win The County Championship six times in the 1930s. Henry Tomlinson established his Anchor brewery on Cherry Street in 1891 and some of his pubs were amongst the most lavishly decorated in the city. Much of the brewery still stands today and is now occupied by a timber yard. The outer wall still bears many distinctive features including the Anchor Brewery sign. The premises were badly damaged in the 1940 blitz. In order to maintain beer supplies to their tied estate, the company merged with the Hope Brewery to form the Hope & Anchor Company. Jubilee Stout was one of the most famous of its lines and rivalled Guinness for its popularity in Yorkshire. Beer making, as well as drinking, has always been popular with the tykes. In 1880 there were 30 major breweries in Sheffield, in addition to many other smaller establishments that produced individual ales. The nature of the working environment meant that steelworkers built up a thirst that became legendary. The 1881 census lists around 1,500 licensed premises.

Bottom left: Pictured c1950, the 346 tram is seen close to the Heavygate Road terminus. This took its name from the Olde Heavy Gate Inn, one of Sheffield's oldest pubs, that was built in 1696. Situated on the Matlock Road at Steel Bank, this hostelry, after various renovations, still attracts those who enjoy a tipple. The tram system is one of the things that most people associate with Sheffield. Steel making and the cutlery trade are the most foremost topics of conversation for outsiders referring to the city, but the trams are also of major interest. When visitors arrive here they soon appreciate that many of the suburbs and surrounding districts are on the hills overlooking the city. They can then appreciate that early motor buses struggled with the gradients and that the railways were only able to serve the valley, meaning that no proper local railway network developed as in other major cities. Tramways were the ideal way to overcome the steep gradients and provide a local transport service. The origin of the tramway can be traced back to the plateways used in mines and quarries to ease the passage of horse-drawn wagons, but the first street tramway in a city was the New York and Harlem line of 1832, coining the term Americans still use today, street railway.

Below: Looking down Waingate from the direction of Haymarket in the July 1959, the Exchange Brewery and Lady's Bridge Hotel buildings that we can see are still with us today. However, they have run the course of their original use. The pub was built for the Tennant's brewery, with which it was directly linked, but taken over by Whitbread in 1962. The brewery closed in the 1980s and the pub, once known as The Brewer on the Bridge, stopped serving in 1993. The shops on the left have disappeared, as have the tramlines. Lady's Bridge has its place in the city's history of public transport. The first route from here to the Golden Ball Hotel, Attercliffe was established in 1873. A move to replace horses with steam power was trialled in 1877 on the Brightside route, but it was not popular as people objected to the smoke and grime. Electricity was a different matter and, in September 1899, a service was begun running from Nether Edge to Tinsley. Receipts in the first year totalled £30,000, but by 1908 had risen to a colossal £285,952 and the age of the tram was well established as a popular and profitable mode of travel. However, by the 1930s some tramway managers were worried men. The initial investment was wearing out and on many systems the profits of the good years had not been reinvested in the trams. Buses and motor cars provided stiff competition with fatal consequences in the postwar era.

Above: Pinstone Street, formerly Pincher Croft Lane and, for a while Pinson Street, was packed for the journey undertaken by last tram to run in Sheffield, or so it was thought at the time. This was the culmination of a special 'last tram week' in early October 1960 and town hall officials, local celebrities and local politicians turned out in force to say goodbye. The public crowded onto the final car and the pavements were thronged by people watching the end of an era. A brass band played lustily to give the service a memorable send off. The first tramway in Sheffield was created under the Tramways Act of 1870, with powers granted in 1872 and the first routes were opened the following year. Rather quaintly, under the legislation of that time, local authorities were precluded from operating tramways, but were empowered to construct them and lease the lines to an individual operating company. Sheffield Tramways Company operated the services, before handing over control to the Corporation that oversaw electrification and expansion of the service. Ironically, less than 35 years after the last tram disappeared, a new supertram service was born. On 21 March 1994 the new breed rattled out of Fitzalan Square and off to Meadowhall. The new system was originally operated by the South Yorkshire Supertram Operating Company, who employed the staff and operated the depot and signalling, but now Stagecoach Supertram is in control.

Right: Tram 134 made its way across Town Hall Square as the camera caught it in its shot towards Barkers Pool and Cinema House. Known as 'The Heart of the City' the area close to here has been revamped in latter years. The Peace Gardens were created as a main public place close to the Town Hall, with Millennium Square just further over. In 1950, the streets were already becoming jammed with an increasing volume of motor cars. The popular trams, forced by their design to follow a rigid route, were slowed in their progress along the streets by cars constantly hogging the tracks in manoeuvres that were both dangerous and time wasting. Eventually, Sheffield moved completely over to buses in 1960, before reintroducing tramways in 1994. Until relocation in 2007, the Sheffield Bus Museum, first opened in 1987, was housed in part of the former Tinsley Tram Shed, demonstrating Sheffield's intriguing transport history. As well as buses, enthusiasts could view various artefacts including destination blinds, tram stops, old road signs, models, timetables and tickets. The former tram depot was the first one built in Sheffield for the Sheffield Tramways Company in 1874. Originally built for the operation of horse trams, the depot was converted for electric operation in 1898-99. Following conversion, the Tinsley depot was capable of accommodating 95 tram cars.

Above: In 1950 we were still in the period after the second world war that has since become known as the time of austerity. Those of us brought up in that era can still recall that rationing of some items was still in force and would not fully disappear for another few years. It was a time when the postwar Labour government made great changes to the way we lived and worked, especially in the fields of the welfare state and nationalisation. These two flagships of the Attlee administration came into force during the late 1940s. The National Health Service, despite the many objections, notably from those GPs who had lucrative practices in the leafy shires, came into being and provided medical care for everyone. No longer did the poorer classes have to rely on homemade remedies or quack prescriptions. There was access to decent treatment for children and assistance and advice on their development. An abiding memory of that time is the delicious taste of the thick, sweet, free baby orange juice and the pink-framed round spectacles worn by shortsighted youngsters. The railways, mines and utility companies were handed over to the state in one of the most swingeing changes any government ever brought about. Here on Union Street, seen from Furnival Street, there was little evidence of any change in the air. It got its name from John Union, a landowner on Brunswick Road who sold off several acres for building purposes in 1866.

Left: Bridge Street and Coulston Street, as viewed from the foot of Snig Hill, have undergone changes as the ring road has been developed since this 1950s' view of the bus terminus was taken. Older readers will recall the clippies, female conductresses, who used to take a passenger's fare and issue him with a ticket. The driver of these buses was in a self contained cab, so he was unable to do anything other than concentrate on the road. Clippies were always much more cheerful than their male counterparts and could be relied on for a cheeky word or two. Light banter between them and their male customers made the journey a much pleasanter experience. Such remarks from a chap as, 'How far do you go, love?' when getting on board would simply get a grin or a, 'Wouldn't you like to know', sort of response. It was harmless fun, but try that today and you would be up before the beak for harassment. Snig Hill has an unusual name and there are several suggestions as to its derivation. One plausible explanation is that a snig was a block of wood put through the wheels of a cart as a form of brake as the slope to the old corn mill at Millsands was rather steep. One dictionary defines it as meaning a small eel, but that would not have had much effect in slowing down a cart!

Above: 'The pig', as this Dennis rescue tender was affectionately known, came into service with Sheffield Fire Brigade in 1934. It was looking fairly careworn by the time it was photographed in the early 1950s. The fire service, in conjunction with the police, now has a museum dedicated to its history in the building that opened as jointly based operations in 1900 at West Bar. Dennis is one of the names that became synonymous with the fire service as the company specialised in this field, though it did diversify into other lines to expand the business. A bicycle company was founded by brothers John and Raymond Dennis in Guildford in 1895 and they soon developed this into a motorbike venture. By 1903, the company was manufacturing cars and buses, soon to be followed by the trademark fire engines that were exported across the world. During the 1914-18 conflict, Dennis Brothers produced lorries and ambulances for use at the front. Continued improvements on its fire engines took place in the 1920s with the adoption of pneumatic tyres and brakes on all four wheels as standard. So that fire crews could dismount easily, most appliances had no enclosed cab and the firemen sat alongside the driver or on a bench along the body side, clinging onto grab rails for grim life.

SHOPPING SPREE

People went about their business in the city centre as seen from on high as we gaze at High Street and Fitzalan Square just a couple of years before the start of World War II. The King's Head and Marples Hotel on the right, with Barclays Bank and the News Theatre in the background, were famous landmarks at the time. The Wine and Spirit Commercial Hotel was established on the corner of the eastern side of High Street in 1870. John Marples took it over in 1886 under a licence granted to the Market Street Wine Vaults and, having undergone a name change to the London Mart, became known to everyone by the family name even though this alteration had not been officially recorded when this photograph was taken. It was a magnificent edifice, rising some seven storeys into the sky, and had its own concert room as well as guestrooms, bars and a grand lounge. As shoppers and office workers scurried along the road, there was much going on across the waters on the Continent. The Spanish Civil War was raging and both Hitler and Mussolini were indulging in the form of sabre rattling that got Prime Minister Neville Chamberlain to embark on his fruitless appeasement mission to Munich in 1938. It was all to no avail, as Sheffield would find out to its cost in the blitz of 1940.

Below: This elevated view of Haymarket, taken on 22 May 1937, just ten days after George VI's coronation, demonstrates how important public transport was to ordinary folk at the time. Although some motor cars can be seen, mainly painted black of course, the number of buses and trams in this shot runs into double figures. These had become the accepted mode of transport since the early years of the 20th century, though the history of the tram system goes back into Victorian times. The first horse drawn service opened in 1873 between Lady's Bridge and Attercliffe, subsequently being extended to Brightside and Tinsley. But, with the coming of electrification and the takeover by the City Corporation, the influence of the tramway spread across all of Sheffield and its suburbs. The ease of getting around brought shoppers into the centre and helped boost retailers' profits, as well a giving the local population the opportunity to visit more easily those friends and relatives who lived a few more miles away. Money was tight during the interwar years as the country felt the after effects of the Great War and the era of depression that followed, but there seem to be plenty of people with a few bob in their pockets in this photograph as the Haymarket looks to have been busy. This street, beneath the former castle walls, was once known as Beast Market, for self explanatory reasons.

Above: Although 1937 was still part of the depression era, some people had money to spend, but they had to be careful. At least at Sheaf Market there was a chance to get some decent produce at a reasonable price. If a housewife waited until near the end of trading for the day she could get even better value for money as traders were anxious to rid themselves of perishable items. This illuminated display by Novel Signs stood over the Broad Street entrance where a cut-out policeman indicated that we should step inside for bargains. The two men at the entrance exemplify the dress code of the day. Even the working classes, as denoted by the flat cape, went out wearing a suit, or jacket and trousers at least. The man standing behind them belonged to a higher social order as he wore a homburg on his head. The Sheaf, or Rag and Tag as it was popularly known, had a number of characters who traded in the market. There were medicine men selling all sorts of potions and cures for any ailment under the sun. Amazingly, these quacks found people gullible enough to believe their claims and part with their hard earned money. Others had goods for sale from the Far East, by which they meant as far east as a little shed in Worksop, or they told fortunes with the promise of a host of tall, dark strangers who were on their way.

Below: It was a busy Saturday afternoon on Angel Street in the late 1940s as locals went about their business in the hope that peacetime would be longlasting. Having spent six war-torn years, everyone was looking forward to a better second half to the century. But, it would be some time coming. Britain's economy had been ravaged by a costly conflict and no longer stood as a major power on the world stage. That role had been taken over by the Americans and their influence in Europe was now established. US troops were in Berlin and their dollars were loaned to their allies under the Marshall Plan, devised by the American Secretary of State, George C Marshall. Permission was given for some $13 billion worth of economic aid, helping to restore industrial and agricultural production, establish financial stability and expand trade. The shoppers on Angel Street did not understand the significance of the pact with America and were just happy to be free from strife. The street takes its name from the Angel Inn, one of Sheffield's foremost pubs. It was referred to in the Burgery accounts as far back as 1682 and was a notable coaching inn before Becoming a temperance house in the early 1900s. It was destroyed in one of the bombing raids in World War II.

Above: This 1948 view of Town Hall Square was taken from Fargate/Barkers Pool. At that time, Fargate extended to Pool Square, not becoming part of Barkers Pool until the 1960s. The Belisha beacon in the foreground helps to date the photograph. This style of crossing, named after the prewar Minister for Transport, Leslie Hore-Belisha, had studs in the road to guide pedestrians across. The now familiar zebra style black and white markings were only introduced in the early 1950s. Britain was in the third year of peace following the defeat of Germany and Japan, but it was still struggling to come to terms with a massive war debt. Additionally, six years of non-investment in industry, added to a need to get on with the physical rebuilding of homes, factories and businesses ripped apart by the bombing campaign of the early 1940s, was costing the country dear. People turned to sport and entertainment as a means of gaining some form of light relief. Cinema audiences were on the up, dance halls were filled every weekend and soccer and cricket stadiums were bursting at the seams. Wilson Peck's music shop on the corner of Leopold Street, still a thriving business today, was a popular retreat for those wishing to entertain themselves. As well as the usual musical instruments, it had a fine range of sheet music. 'Once in love with Amy' by Dean Martin was one of the best sellers.

Below: A map of 1736 shows part of this area as Prior Gate, but most historians regard that as inaccurate and feel that it has always been High Street. Whatever its designation, this part of the city has always been a busy spot. This general view from the mid 1950s gives quite a fascinating insight into attitudes and standards of half a century and more ago, particularly when applied to fashion. Many of the younger women are in mid calf length dresses, a complete turn around from a decade before when cloth was in short supply and rationed, thus dictating hem lengths. Many more mature women had come to the city wearing their hats as they felt undressed or far too casually turned out to be seen bareheaded. Most men had similar conservative ideas. Few ventured out without donning a jacket, collar and tie and the older generation often sported the flat caps that tended to amuse snooty southerners. Today, High Street is part of the main supertram route through Sheffield and there is no chance that we will see cars parked on the highway as we do here. With the number of people out and about on the streets it certainly seems we are in the period of economic recovery that followed the austere postwar years and led Prime Minister Macmillan to inform us that 'we have never had it so good'.

In the early 1950s the pony and trap was still a feature on our roads, though its use had been in decline since well before the second world war. The duo on board this one, looking onto Broad Street from Sheaf Street, seems to be indulging itself in some form of trotting race, perhaps imagining that they are at the reins of a sulky on some American racetrack. A whitecoated bobby has just waved them on and the drivers are repeating a manoeuvre they must have carried out countless times before. However, as the level of traffic on the roads increased at a pace during the 1950s, the days of their mode of transport for themselves and their goods as a viable way of getting around would soon draw to a close. Sheaf Market is to the left, with Castlefolds to the right. An Act of Parliament, made in 1847, authorised construction of a new market hall between Castle Folds and Dixon Lane for the sale of general produce. Land around the new hall, between Exchange Street and Broad Street, was to be cleared for stalls and fairs, while the Green Market, by now almost solely used for the sale of fish, would be discontinued once the new hall was opened. This same authorisation led the way for the creation of Castlefolds Market on land between the Corn Exchange and Norfolk Market Hall.

Below: Once known as Bull Stake, possibly after the practice of bull baiting that was once a questionable entertainment for our ancestors, the name was changed in the 1830s to Haymarket. This reflected one of the Duke of Norfolk family's several unsuccessful attempts to establish a corn and hay market in the city. Looking towards Fitzalan Square in 1961, the new Woolworth's is in the process of construction. Every town and city in the land has at least one of this chain of cheap and cheerful stores on its streets. The original five and ten cent store came across the Atlantic to Britain in 1909, opening its first branch in Liverpool. Why was it though, back in the 1960s, that the girls at the till always seemed to have the stock phrase, 'How much is it, love?' whenever you presented an intended purchase to them. Other premises we can see here include Arthur Davy and Sons, Sheffield's leading grocer especially noted for his pork products. The Mikado Café can be seen, along with Weaver to Wearer. This latter retailer referred to itself as 'tailor to the modern world' and was a rival to the likes of Burton's and John Collier. At the time of this photograph men's tailoring was big business for the chain stores and each had its own catchy slogan. Burton was 'the tailor of taste' and John Collier had 'the window to watch'.

Above: Sheaf Market, seen in this elevated view of Broad Street that was taken in 1970, can trace its roots back to 1296 when Edward I granted a charter to Thomas de Furnival to hold markets and an annual fair in the town. For the next six centuries the markets were owned, operated and developed by the lords of the manor. Not a bad little earner, as someone once said. Sheffield Corporation purchased the markets and rights in 1899 from the then lord, Henry, 15th Duke of Norfolk, for the not inconsiderable sum of £526,000. From the start of the 14th century, a market was held on the Tuesday of each week and a fair took place every year during the three days of the feast of the Holy Trinity. In 1847 a Parliamentary Act led to the creation of Castlefolds Markets, on land between the Corn Exchange and the Norfolk Market Hall. The Sheaf Open Market was also established on the adjacent site and became popularly known as 'the Rag and Tag market'. In 1973, the opening of Sheaf Market Hall replaced the adjoining Rag and Tag Market and with it went the last surviving relic of the original 19th century undertaking. In 1996, exactly 700 years after the granting of the market charter, the City Council announced plans for the major redevelopment of Castlegate Markets.

AT WORK

Left: These Edwardian ladies stood outside L and A Wilkinson's, then owned by James Wilkinson, a bookseller and stationer who had extended the scope of this pitch in Norfolk Market by becoming an agent for Edison's phonographs and records. This was right at the start of a new industry and must have been an exciting period for those involved. Thomas Alva Edison was the quintessential American inventor in the era of Yankee ingenuity. He was responsible for the production of transmitters, microphones, incandescent lamps, a form of electric railway, generators and a myriad of other things. He filed over 1,000 patents, including one for the phonograph in 1877. The first recordings were made on cylinders, but the discs or records that Emile Berliner brought out in 1887 gradually took over the market. By the early 1900s, these were still a luxury item for most households and became something of a status symbol, but eventually mass production brought the phonograph or gramophone into many homes. These women in Norfolk Market would have enjoyed Marie Lloyd's rendition of 'The boy I love is up in the gallery' or 'Oh Mr Porter', but perhaps they had a more classical ear and liked 'Cielo e mar' or fancied a lively number such as Scott Joplin's 'Maple Leaf Rag'.

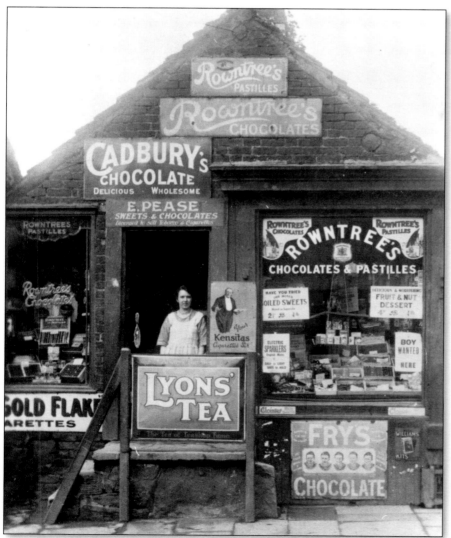

Left: A trip along Chesterfield Road in the mid 1920s would have brought you to Woodseats and, believe it or not, Ye Olde Sweete Shop. This little establishment also sold tobacco and tea, but mainly concentrated on confectionery sales. Fry's Five Boys was just one of the lines being advertised. The picture of these lads was first used on Fry's milk chocolate bars in 1902 and the product was not withdrawn from production until 1976. The images of the boys supposedly told a story of desperation, pacification, expectation, acclamation, and realisation that … it's Fry! The photographs were taken by Messrs Poulton and Son and the model for all five was the photographer's own son, Lindsay. A rag soaked in ammonia was used to achieve the desperation face. Imagine how social services would react to that story today. An advertisement for Kensitas cigarettes shows a butler offering a packet on a tray, suggesting that it was an upmarket smoke. However, J Wix, the company manufacturing this brand, had its eye on both ends of the social market. In 1926 it introduced a coupon scheme in its packets and in 1933 began producing cigarette cards with a difference - woven silk flowers!

Below: Workmates can be great pals who stay with you for life. After all, when you spend eight hours on a shift in close proximity with others, you just have to get on to make the day go well. This group of polishers at Stainless Plating Ltd look very happy. Perhaps the women had just knocked off for the day. Certainly, they are blessed with the sunniest of smiles and perhaps some of their delight came from the knowledge of a job well done. There are two main forms of chrome plating. The bright chrome plating process typically places a 10 micrometre layer over a nickel plate, imparting a mirror like finish to such items as automobile trims and furniture frames. Thicker deposits, that can be as dense as 1,000 micrometres, are called hard chrome and used in industrial equipment that has a heavy work load. These ladies probably did not know it, but their industry had its problems with health issues. Over exposure to chromium could lead to nasal problems, ulcers and even lung cancer. Many chrome plating shops are small operations that have been in business for many years and may be located in close proximity to residences or schools. Stainless Plating, in common with many of its competitors, came under pressure in the early 1990s from new environmental legislation. Having also outgrown its premises, it relocated from the city centre to the Lower Don Valley.

Right: During the last war a number of evening play centres were established where children from homes affected by bomb damage could come and spend some time in meaningful activities. For girls this meant traditional activities related to the home and here they could practise their needlecraft skills. The sewing machine was one of the almost mandatory accessories that any woman would possess in those days. Everyone was more than capable of running up a pair of curtains, making a dress or mending damaged clothing. In fact, a 'make do and mend' campaign was officially launched in 1943 with the issuing of a government booklet. Cloth was urgently needed to kit out the armed forces and it was heavily rationed at home. A housewife couldn't replace household furnishings or create new clothes as she could in the past, and to save important clothing ration coupons the guide was produced by the Ministry of Information. It gave useful advice on how to extend the life of clothes, sheets, curtains and tablecloths and how to recycle damaged and worn clothing and soft furnishings. The ideal housewife, known as Mrs. Sew and Sew, featured in advertisements and women's magazines as well as in cinema shorts. However, to working class women, who had always had to make do and mend even before rationing was introduced, this was nothing new and seemed all very patronising.

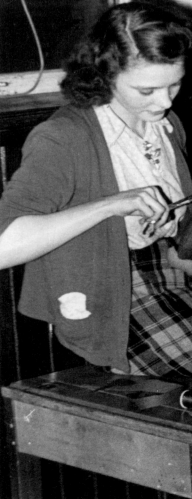

Left: Is great granny, sitting over in the corner with her knitting, one of these pupils who went to Hucklow Road Infant School in 1931? Is she, perhaps, your partner across the table at the local bridge club where she ruffs opponents' aces with a gleeful look in her eye? Could it be that the great grandpa who is always telling the little ones jokes is the widely grinning lad on the second row back? He was always a comedian, then. No doubt Miss Dorothy Shaw kept him in place, because teachers were both feared and respected back then. They stood no nonsense, however demure they looked. Even as young children, this class knew that any transgression would bring a quick smack across the legs or a stroke of the cane for really naughty behaviour, but those children who were in her class still recall the woman who gave them such a good start in life.

George Smith was a master cutler in the mid 18th century. He had a large family of 10 children and they and 12 apprentices all lived in a large house in Peacroft. One of his sons rose to become the headmaster of Sheffield Free Grammar School and the family name lives on in the designation of Smithfield, a small back street off the A61, not far from West Bar. Looking towards the Phoenix Foundry, Snow Lane we can see a number of locals lounging against the walls. This was the era of the depression and the early 1930s was not a time that the working classes found easy. There was no such thing as the welfare state and unemployment reached three million at one stage. Life at the bottom end of society was a struggle to make ends meet and pushed even the mildest mannered into forceful protest. In 1936, a march of unemployed men from Jarrow in the northeast made its way to London, but their pleas fell upon deaf ears. The Phoenix Foundry was part of a long history in Sheffield's steelmaking pedigree. During the 15th century the streams that converge on the city began to be used for power for grinding and forging operations. Benjamin Huntsman developed the crucible process of steelmaking, thereby obtaining a reliable product that by 1830 had earned Sheffield recognition as the world centre of high-grade steel manufacture.

Below: In the 1940s, Butler the cutler was a common sight in the city suburbs. He offered a rather bizarre mix of services. As well as the orthodox knife and razor sharpening that he could perform, Butler also provided a line in repairing umbrellas. Barrows and carts, whether hand drawn or using actual horse power, were frequent enough not to provoke comment well into the second half of the last century. Window cleaners went on their rounds happily pushing a cart that had a ladder, bucket and chamois on board. Of course, it was always irritating when they asked for a clean bucket of water just after they had finished doing your windows. The rag and bone man could be heard streets away as his loud cries marked his imminent arrival. He would take virtually anything you wanted to get rid of, but its value seldom changed. Whatever the items, they were worth a donkeystone. Housewives were happy enough with the exchange as the front step had to be done. Whatever amount of time she had spare from washing, cooking, mending and cleaning there had to be enough to devote to that threshold, for it would never do if Mrs Ecclestone at No 9, her of the lace curtains and bay window, had a brighter front step. Rhubarb and rose growers were also glad to see the horse and cart arrive.

Sheffield Forgemasters - Successor to a Steel and Engineering Dynasty

Today Sheffield Forgemasters is at the forefront of the worldwide heavy engineering industry. It is the successor to such famous Sheffield names as Vickers, English Steel, Firth Brown and British Steel.

The origins of the company go back to the 1750s. However it was Edward Vickers, a traditional miller owning a water mill on Millsands, close to the centre of Sheffield, together with other members of his and the Naylor family who had iron and steel interests, who really set the foundations for the business in 1805.

Sheffield showed its mettle (and its metal) at the Great exhibition of 1851, Vickers making a 'monster' steel ingot (the largest ever at that time) weighing in at 24cwts. So many crucible heats were required for the ingot (over 40) that other works in the Millsands area were needed to contribute by wheeling crucibles of molten steel along the street. Molten steel still crosses Brightside Lane at Forgemasters River Don Works – but now in 95 tonne quantities!

In 1856 Henry Bessemer patented the first bulk steel-making process whereby several tons of steel could be produced in less than one hour. Within a few years bulk steel production would be the city's mainstay. John Brown built the Atlas Works on farmland immediately east of the city, closely followed by Vickers with its giant River Don Works in 1865.

Vickers had the largest crucible melting shop able to pour a 20 ton piece. Today Forgemasters still produces the largest forgings and castings in the western world – only now 600 tonnes of steel can be poured to make a 350 tonne casting.

Cast steel bells were a significant product and Vickers exported them around the world – they were much cheaper than the traditional bronze variety. A peal of such bells hangs in Sheffield's millennium gallery. The largest bell ever made at River Don was the 74inch San Francisco fire bell weighing nearly two and a half tons.

In 1850 Sheffield produced some 35,000 tons of steel – over half of world production. Within 15 years, Sheffield was still making over half of the world's steel but now it was well over one million tons annually! In the 1860s Tom Vickers designed the giant crucible melt shop, developed the Mayer moulding method for castings and installed one of the first Siemens open hearth melting

Top: *Naylor Vickers Millsands Works, Sheffield in 1830.*
Below left: *Pouring a large casting from a multitude of crucible melts in 1875 (courtesy of Sheffield Industrial Museums Trust).* **Below:** *Molten Steel still crosses Brightside Lane – but in ladles of 95t.*

During the late 19th century Tom Vickers made many major technological developments whilst his brother Albert was the businessman. Vickers also had the most successful arms salesman ever in Basil Zaharoff who earned commissions that would today be worth many £millions.

Through the 1890s, Vickers, Cammells and Browns all had massive forging presses to form armour plate, some of it up to a foot thick. Following the amalgamation into Vickers in 1897 of Armstrong Whitworth and the Barrow shipyard, the company became dominant worldwide and various subsidiaries and joint ventures appeared as far apart as Canada and Japan. In 1905 Cammells laid down a new armour plate mill at Grimesthorpe capable of rolling a 90 ton ingot into plate. The steam engine to drive this was made by Davy at Darnall and was one of the most powerful ever made – and can still be seen operating in the Kelham Island museum.

furnaces for quality bulk steel. That was followed in 1882 by the first heavy forging press.

Much of Vickers success was due to demand from the USA for railroad equipment. Yet this business was to be soon lost due to the massive new US facilities such as those of Carnegie in Pittsburgh.

Sheffield was resilient and realised it needed to get closer to end products to make profits again. Both Vickers at River Don Works and Browns at Atlas Works became two of the world's leading producers of armaments. Vickers also diversified into shipbuilding with the acquisition of a shipyard at Barrow to build 'ironclads', dreadnoughts and, through the Nordenfeld connection, the world's first submarine. Sheffield Forgemasters continues as the supplier of critical items for Britain's nuclear submarine construction programme.

By 1870 the River Don Works was one of the two largest engineering steel enterprises in the world rivalled only by Bochum in Germany – both specialising in railway, marine and armament work – but from 1888 Vickers had the edge. Naval guns were largely unchanged since Trafalgar, but now Armstrong's rifled naval gun made most of the fleet obsolete. Both Vickers and Firth Brown moved into the manufacture of armour plate. Vickers' portfolio also included the innovative Maxim machine gun.

Top: *Rolling Armour Plate during the visit of HM Queen Victoria in 1897.* *Right:* *Armour plate Mill in the 1950s powered by the Steam Engine now in Kelham Island Museum*

Harry Brearley is famous for the invention of stainless steel in 1913. Firth Brown was intent on developing improved alloys for gun barrels and one failed high-chrome trial left to the elements for some weeks did not rust. Brearley gave samples to friends to forge into cutlery blades – and the rest is history.

The first world war meant peak production. But over 1,000 of the River Don workforce joined up with the Sheffield 'pals' and production was severely curtailed. Sadly many pals never returned.

Post-war the great depression of the 1920s forced rationalisation. English Steel was the result of a merger with Cammell Laird and the Vickers Group; Firth Brown was also consolidated. Vickers embarked on a major reinvestment programme in the 1930s.

the new open-hearth melting shop, there is the story of his meeting a first-hand melter. Nobody except directors were meant to speak with the King who was rather shy. However the King approached the melter with a question. This giant of a man put his arm around the diminutive King saying, 'Si thee King, tha' knows tha' just.......' The King, grateful for the detailed explanation, rejoined the party, much to the consternation of the assembled hierarchy!

After the war the business developed a new range products including turbine rotors and boiler drums for power stations and ships, railway suspensions and couplers, high performance rolling mill rolls and other steelplant products as well as components for the world's first nuclear power station at Calder Hall.

Political interference was to dog the industry for years in the shape of nationalisation twice. The planned move of the River Don Works to the new site at Tinsley Park was shelved in 1965.

The River Don Works was renationalised in 1967 into British Steel. In 1972 British Steel did a deal with Firth Brown whereby the entire alloy forging business from ingots below 70 tonnes was exchanged for Firth Brown's interest in the stainless plant on Shepcote Lane. BSC then redeveloped the stainless flat product business which is now part of Outokompu. The general expectation was that this would see the slow demise of the rest of the River Don business. However against the odds, new business was developed including castings for the offshore oil industry. The prototype casting is now displayed outside the works on the Forgemasters traffic island.

World War II saw output reach new heights. The River Don Works was a key target - though largely missed - in the Sheffield blitz. This was very fortuitous as the only forge able to produce crankshafts for the Merlin engine which powered both Spitfire and Lancaster aircraft remained unscathed. The Grimesthorpe foundry produced Barnes Wallace's bouncing bombs of Dambusters fame and also the largest-ever conventional 'grand slam' bomb at 10 tons, used to destroy V2 sites.

The strategic importance of Sheffield steel was emphasised by illustrious visitors such as Winston Churchill to the River Don Works. During one visit by George VI to open

Top: Winston Churchill inspecting Armament Production (inset) at River Don Works during WW II.
*Above: HM Queen Elisabeth & Prince Philip visiting River Don Works in October 1954. **Right:** Eager anticipation for the Royal Visitors.*

Despite the extra business and suffering from an asset stripping management, Firth Brown was facing failure by 1981. Mrs Thatcher's first steel privatisation was close to being jeopardised and it was not an option for BSC to acquire an ailing competitor. BSC supported Firth Brown with orders until the amalgamation with the River Don Works to form the private sector company, Sheffield Forgemasters, could be concluded.

Prior to formation, Firth Brown had to make 1,000 redundancies from its 4,000 workforce. Thus Sheffield Forgemasters came into being in 1983 with a total workforce of 6,500, only a fifth of what both companies had together employed some 20 years earlier. In less than three years however, despite an annual turnover of £100m, the new company was losing around £20m per annum.

One Friday in 1984, shareholders of Forgemasters (BSC and FB) wrote off their investments, fired the entire board and brought in new management headed by Phillip

Wright. At a meeting with management on the following Monday afternoon he outlined a survival plan. Two latecomers to the meeting were told to collect their P45s! The militant South Yorkshire trade unionism that had so damaged other poorly-managed steel companies was still alive and within a few months a protracted strike on the Atlas site focussed minds. The outcome ultimately ensured the survival and success of the business. The castings company, River Don Castings, achieved almost break-even in its first year of operation with just 134 people compared with over 400 the previous year for the same turnover of £5m when it had lost over £2m.

With BSC itself about to be privatised in 1987, Sheffield Forgemasters' management agreed a management buy-out (MBO). The company's success

Top: *World class production in the 1960s.*
Above: *Siemens Open Hearth Steel Furnaces in 1950s.*
Left: *1950s Works Transport.*

aerospace business to Allegheny Teledyne, and the River Don and Rolls businesses to Atchison Castings. Atchison's management failed to develop their business and in 2003 their whole enterprise went into liquidation. Fortunately, a major turnaround at River Don enabled local management led by Graham Honeyman to ring-fence that business from administration. After two years of patient progress to overcome major hurdles including a difficult market and pension problems, management was able to complete an MBO.

Today the company, now in its third century and probably the oldest steel business in the world, remains at the forefront of technology for castings and forgings for its heavy engineering customers across the world.

Top: Forging a large hollow shaft in the 1950s.
Below: The first cast steel node developed for offshore platforms in 1978 now displayed outside the works on the Forgemasters island. ***Bottom left:*** 1950s style Christmas lunch for the Works Management. ***Bottom right:*** The largest casting made in the Western World at almost 350 tonnes in 2006.

through the next decade bucked the trend by dramatic increases in export sales. Queen's Awards for Technology and Export were received.

Following on from earlier castings business in Iraq, an order for some 50 alloy-steel 'pressure tubes' to exacting standards was secured with the support of DTI. It was only much later that suspicions were raised regarding the true use for these items – and by that time the Government had changed sides! The contract ensured that everything was paid for before the items left Sheffield - only to be impounded at the docks and various Forgemasters executives arrested for a day. Clips of the Forgemasters video were shown on TV news programmes around the world - and significant new business enquiries were generated! The subsequent Scott inquiry into the 'super-gun' affair exonerated Forgemasters.

The uncertainty hanging over the company delayed interesting business opportunities but in 1998 the company was sold in two parts to USA buyers – the

Shepherd Distribution Services Sheffield - A Winning Business

NEW premises for J. J. Shepherd

J. J. SHEPHERD

Our spacious new premises are the most up to date in Yorkshire. To assure you of prompt and efficient delivery, our large fleet of vehicles is regularly maintained in first class condition. Storage space available.

Vehicles up to SIXTEEN TONS capacity

Serving the
**MIDLANDS,
NORTH EAST,
LONDON, GLASGOW
SOUTH WALES**
and all **PORTS**

J. J. SHEPHERD (Est. 1946) LTD. ★ Haulage Contractors

LOW ROAD, OUGHTIBRIDGE.   Telephones Oughtibridge 2271/2/3.

With a history going back more than six decades Shepherd Distribution Services has built its reputation on offering its customers solutions to their distribution problems. Today the company's fleet of over 50 vehicles and its comprehensive warehousing facilities offers clients a unique range of nationwide distribution options.

Since the late 80s Shepherds have been well know locally for their expertise in the collection, handling and delivery of all manner of awkwardly shaped general engineering and industrial products in small or part-load consignments. Shepherds deliver more than 1,500 tonnes of this type of goods, made up of some 2,500 collections and deliveries, nationally every single week.

Over the past 10 years, however, they have also become a leading player in the nationwide distribution of 1-3 pallet consignments of all types of consumer goods through its involvement with the Palletline network.

JJ Shepherd (Est. 1946) Ltd was formed, as its name implies, in 1946 by Jack Shepherd as a full load steel and refractory industries haulier. The firm was based at Church Street, Oughtibridge. It was the first year of peace after six years of world war. A new Labour Government had been elected only twelve months previously, and with it came the promise of nationalisation of the coal and steel industries alongside the railways. Nationalisation too was promised for the road transport industry, but there would still be room for small road hauliers to operate and, if they were good enough and tough enough, to thrive.

In those days lorry drivers had to be tough. Power steering may have been invented in the 1920s, and commercially available since the 1950s, but neither it nor air-assisted clutches and gear changes were yet to be found amongst the transport fleets of Britain.

But if the job was tough Jack Shepherd was more than equal to the challenge. In the post-war years Sheffield was very busy moving massive quantities of steel and by the 1960s Shepherd's had became one of the largest and most successful hauliers in the area.

In 1963 the company moved to premises on Low Road, Oughtibridge. By now the company was working flat out for the likes of Dunford and Elliot, Brown Bailey Steels, Osbourne Hadfields, WT Flather, and Habershon Steel Strip.

Above: The company advertise the new premises in the *Sheffield Star in November 1963.*
Above right and right: *JJ Shepherd's Low Road, Oughtibridge premises in the mid 1960s.*

The new depot on Low Road was 'state of the art' for it's time, and included its own four-bay garage workshop and a 25,000 sq ft warehouse.

The opening years of the 1970s however were amongst the least propitious in the 20th century for road transport. Many haulage firms in this period failed to see the end of the decade let alone the 21st century.

Inflation, which would soon peak at almost 30 per cent, would be the least of the transport industry's problems.

Far more serious was the Oil Crisis, an event which plunged the whole world economy into chaos.

The crisis began in October 1973 when the Arab oil-producing states decided to simultaneously restrict oil production and raise prices. The original reason for doing this was as a short–term political weapon in the Arab-Israeli War, but it was soon seen as a way of raising vast revenues.

Over three months the oil producing countries raised their take on each barrel of oil from $1.75 to $7.00. In a year the price of oil imported into Britain rose almost threefold. Inevitably the price of petrol and diesel rose in response. For some time fuel rationing became a real possibility.

As a direct result of the Oil Crisis the world economy moved into recession.

Not until 1976 would Britain and the world's economy begin to stabilise, helped by the welcome arrival of North Sea oil production in 1975.

For many businesses, especially those in the transport industry this period of economic 'stagflation' as it became known was their death knell.

Yet 'when the going gets tough the tough get going' and Shepherd's weathered the storm.

Company founder Jack Shepherd died in the late 1980s and his son Ray took on the management of the company. At this point in the company's history the fleet consisted of around 35 vehicles, mainly ERF, Albion and Leylands.

During the 1980s however, despite surviving the 1970s, the company fell on hard times with the decline in the huge volume of steel which had previously flowed from Sheffield's steel mills. It was touch and go whether or not the firm would survive.

The Thatcher years saw a major restructuring of British industry as Margaret Thatcher's Conservative government forced painful changes to the economy of the United Kingdom. The coal and steel industries which had flourished under nationalisation after the second world war were now left to sink or swim. Mostly they sank, and alongside them many firms which had relied on those industries as major customers.

By the end of the decade it was obvious that a new strategy would have to be devised if the company was to avoid going into liquidation. Happily Ray Shepherd now saw a new market for the company in the provision of nation-wide delivery service for the local steel stockholders rather than the steel producers. Typically this involved delivery of not the 20 tonnes of steel for one delivery point as had previously been the case, but several 'part loads' of steel of general engineering products amounting to 20 tonnes in

total. The average 'drop weight' was about three tonnes and the vehicle revenue was far greater - though the increased overheads due to the cost of collection and handling needed to be watched closely if profitability was to be maintained.

Top and above: Low Road in the 1980s (top) and 1990s. *Right:* A Shepherd double deck trailer in the Palletline livery.

In response to changing needs three quarters of the firm's fleet of maximum-weight articulated lorries were now replaced by more flexible 4 and 10 tonne carrying vehicles. Overhead cranes were installed in the warehouse at Low Road, and a night loading shift was started.

The new 'groupage' system revolved around vehicles collecting all manner of steel and engineering-related products from the South Yorkshire area during the daytime. These goods were then 'consolidated' back at the Low Road depot where they were loaded overnight on to vehicles to deliver in the relevant areas the following day.

Shepherd's staff's detailed knowledge of their customers' products gave the company a massive edge over the competition. Equally the company's ability to handle all manner of steel-related products with its advanced handling equipment made the nightly loading process a highly efficient and streamlined operation.

The company turned the corner in the second half of the 1980s due to the new strategy which was driven hard by Ray Shepherd, yet even so more major change was in the offing for the business. In 1991 a management buy out saw the controlling interest in the company change hands. Paul Tilley joined the company with a background in business development in the transport industry and he, together with Ian Wood and Trevor Hirst, embarked on the next stage of the company's development.

With the new team in place it soon became clear that the Low Road site was far too small for the company's ambitious plan. Accordingly a trawl of South Yorkshire's available sites was carried out, but with little success – every site inspected would turn out to be too small or too large or in the wrong location.

During the course of those prolonged investigations another local haulier expressed interest in being bought out by Shepherd's. The haulier was suffering in the harsh economic climate then prevailing, and with an ageing fleet of vehicles in urgent need of replacement he was not too far a way from liquidation. The main attraction of the firm for Shepherd's however, was not its vehicles, but rather the fact that it possessed a large site from which Shepherd's could develop and grow its 'groupage' operation.

Discussions were at an advanced stage for the acquisition of the struggling haulage firm and its large site when in 1993 news came that RDB Freightlines Ltd, which was generally acknowledged to be Shepherd's main competitor in the groupage market, was going into liquidation.

At that time RDB had a national network of depots and a turnover of more than £12 million per annum – four times the size of Shepherd's business. Like Shepherd's RDB too had undergone a management buy out earlier in the year, so it was rather puzzling that all could have gone wrong so quickly.

RDB's Sheffield operating base was on Birley Vale Avenue in Intake, a three and a half acre site which seemed huge compared to Shepherd's base at Low Road. Shepherd's contacted the Receiver and was quoted a sale price for the RDB site in excess of £1 million – far beyond Shepherds' reach. The dilemma now facing the management team was whether to continue with the attempt to acquire the ailing haulier or continue to negotiate with the RDB's Receiver – clearly the firm could not do both. In the end Shepherds opted for what turned out to be a fairly long-winded negotiation to buy RDB's Birley Vale Avenue site. The deal was finally done for £450,000, a far better price than the million pounds plus first suggested.

The new site consisted of two 30,000 sq ft warehouses, plus extensive office space on the 3.5 acre site. One warehouse was specifically designed for handling long steel products with six overhead cranes, whilst the other was designed for handling pallets. The site was a quantum leap forward in size and facilities compared to Low Road. In an instant Shepherds had seen the demise of its main competitor, bought up its vastly more efficient operating

Above: Full maintenance of the fleet.
Below: The warehousing facility at Shepherd's.

base, acquired a significant number of its customers and elevated itself into the big league.

These were heady times indeed for three lads who had just invested every last penny they had in a non-too secure transport business during one of the worst industrial climates for years. But fortune favours the brave.

Paul Tilley tells the tale of standing in the hot dog queue at the auction of the RDB fleet and listening to two people in the queue expressing the view that it was 'a big site' and that 'they wouldn't fancy trying to make it pay'. Knowing that the Shepherds deal with the Receiver was just about to be completed the pessimistic comment did nothing to improve Paul's appetite.

Appetites would however quickly return, along with a taste for innovation and progress.

In 1995 Shepherds invested in the then fledgling 'Palletline' network. Palletline is a network of hauliers based throughout the United Kingdom who joined together. Each carrier trunks its customers' pallets to a central hub in Birmingham on a nightly basis and collects pallets for delivery to their own local postcode areas next day. At Shepherd's, accredited to ISO 9002 in 1994, quality service is assured from collection to delivery. On receipt of

goods into the company's warehouses all consignment are checked in order to ensure absolute correctness. Any discrepancies are notified to customers immediately. From receipt to delivery all goods are traceable at all times – and with all vehicles fitted with cab communication systems contact can be made with drivers in the event of changing circumstances.

Pallet networks were at that time a fairly new phenomenon largely born out of the needs of an industry generally populated by small hauliers. Joining together in this way even small operators were able to offer their customers a truly nationwide delivery service for one to three pallet consignments.

Small however, was no longer a word which could be applied to Shepherd's. The company's transport fleet by now approaching 60 strong, though it was still virtually all flat-beds. By investing in Palletline Shepherd's had the opportunity to enter markets previously unavailable to it due to its fleet profile: once again, spotting a business opportunity, the company took on a new dimension.

Palletline was the first pallet network, and has since been imitated but never equalled. It still remains the best and most respected network in the United Kingdom. In 1995 Palletline was handling fewer than 1,000 pallets a night. In 2006 Palletline was handling up to 9,000 nightly through its central hub in Birmingham and its two regional hubs in London and Preston.

Shepherd's would become a major contributor to that phenomenal growth. The company by now had been renamed Shepherd Distribution Services to more accurately reflect the broader service offered. Shepherd's would see its annual sales rise to a figure in excess of £6 million – and with healthy profits. The workforce supporting its now substantial fleet of vehicles numbers 125.

Today, more than sixty years after its founding by Jack Shepherd in 1946, his successors in the company have turned the business into an exceptional multi-faceted organisation providing not just distribution services but also storage facilities and third party contract distribution services. A truly remarkable achievement.

Above: Shepherd's, Birley Vale Avenue, mid 1990s.
Below: Three of the company's latest model Volvo's which went on the road in January 2007.

Wortley Hall - An Oasis of Socialism

W hy should only the wealthy occupy grand houses? In 1950 a group of people within the trade union, Labour Party and Co-operative movements from throughout South Yorkshire decided to lease a stately home for everyone to use.

Launching a national appeal for donations the group held a St Leger draw and sold 'shilling shares' to raise the cash needed to lease, and subsequently buy, Wortley Hall near Sheffield.

Today there is a widespread misunderstanding as to who owns and controls Wortley Hall. Many think it is owned by the Labour Party, others the TUC or some other trade

union or co-operative organisation. In fact, when it was decided to take over the Hall a completely new and independent co-operative organisation was set up known as Wortley Hall (Labour's Home).

Those who bought the one shilling (5p) shares became the collective owners. Both institutions and individuals could buy the shares, though each shareholder had to be an organisation, or associated with an organisation, connected with the trade union movement, the Labour Party, Co-operative movement or other socialist-inspired body.

All shareholders, whether institutions or individuals, would each have equal standing. Today a minimum investment of £5 (one share) is required, with no maximum holding for organisations, but with a limit of £200 (40 shares) for individuals. Shareholders include people from

Top: *The beautiful Wortley Hall Country Mansion.*
Above right: *The old servants' bell board.*
Left: *A dinner in 1951.*

the broadest base within the Labour movement: women and men of all ages, from many different jobs and professions, as well as many MPs, MEPs and full time trade union officers. Probably every TUC-recognised trade union is represented by either holding shares or by members of those unions holding shares.

Each shareholder, whether an organisation or an individual, has just one vote at the Annual Meeting where Officers are elected consisting of a Management Board of 12 and a President elected to serve for two years, and a Members Committee of 20, each of whom serves for one year. A Political Secretary is elected for a five year period.

With the success of the fund raising drive volunteers began descending on the Hall and grounds in late 1950 to prepare it for use as an educational holiday home.

Above: An aerial view of Wortley Hall and grounds.
Below: London Unity Theatre present a performance of The Ragged Trousered Philanthropists at Wortley Hall in 1954.

Wortley Hall became a beautiful and much loved oasis of socialism. The once neglected grounds now reflect the devotion of the Hall's gardeners, whilst indoors many changes would be made to make it today's popular venue for conferences, schools meetings, dinners and weddings. All 49 bedrooms are en-suite.

Wortley Hall's story of course goes back much further than 1950. Wortley is the family name of the Earls of Wharncliffe. Alunus de Wortley is recorded as having his residence at Wortley in the Pipe Rolls of 1165. He was followed by seven successive Nicholas de Wortleys who were Lords of the Manor of Wortley. Sir Thomas Wortley, born in 1440, lived at 'The Manor' Wortley, presumed to be Wortley Hall, until he built Wharncliffe Lodge in 1510.

Thomas Wortley's great grandson, Sir Richard Wortley, rebuilt Wortley Hall in 1586; later it seems he got into debt and his estates were sequestered. Sir Richard died in 1603 and his widow remarried, becoming the Countess of Devonshire. The Countess bought back the estates in 1643 and settled them on her grandson Sir Francis Wortley II.

Sir Francis Wortley I was created the first baronet by James I and he took the side of the Loyalists in the Civil War of 1642-48.

In that period Wortley Hall was turned into a fortress. Sir Francis Wortley commanded the Loyalist garrison at Tankersley and led the Loyalists at the battle of Tankersley Moor; alas he was taken prisoner by the Roundheads and transferred to the Tower of London.

Sir Francis Wortley II eventually passed the Wortley estates to his natural daughter, Ann Newcomen. She married Sidney Montagu, the second son of the Earl of Sandwich, but the couple did not live at Wortley Hall.

Ann and Sidney's son Edward, who had taken the Wortley surname, began to rebuild the Hall in 1743. The architect chosen was John Platt of Rotherham with the whole work intended to be completed by 1761. The South front of the house was built in 1743-46 by Giacomo Leoni, with the east wing being added about 15 years later.

However, it would take rather longer than 18 years to make the house entirely habitable: in 1800 James Archibald Stuart Wortley, first Baron Wharncliffe, and his wife Lady Caroline Creighton should have taken up residence - but discovered they were unable to do so because for some reason the builders had omitted to include a staircase!

The landscaping, ornamental planting and the ultimate beauty of the gardens is attributed to the work of Lady Caroline.

Subsequently that early 19th century park was progressively improved. WS Gilpin is said to have been involved in the work as was Joseph Harrison, head gardener in the mid 19th century. Prior to the publication of Harrison's 'Gardener and Foresters Record' and his 'Floricultural Cabinet' in 1833, gardening information and news passed only by word of mouth from head gardener to head gardener.

Leading Sheffield artist, Geoffrey Sykes, was commissioned in the early 1860s to design and paint the ceiling of the Salon (today the Foundry Dining Room); when Sykes died the work was completed by Sir John Pointer. Thereafter however, the Hall went into decline.

From 1939-45, during the second world war, parts of the Hall were occupied by the army, and after 1945 the unoccupied Hall began to fall into disrepair. The gardens were overgrown with weeds and the grass knee high. By

Top left: Jack & Doris Matthewman with Mick & Mary Shaw at the 50th Anniversary Celebrations of Wortley Hall 'Labour's Home'. **Top right:** *Former President, Stuart Charnley, left, with Michael Clapham MP (for Barnsley West and Penistone) and his wife Yvonne, pictured at the celebrations to mark the 50th Anniversary of Wortley Hall 'Labour's Home'.* **Left** *Two views showing the beauty of Wortley Hall.*

1949 half the Salon ceiling's ornamental design had been obliterated by damp: it would take immense efforts to eventually restore one of the finest Renaissance-style ceiling decorations in Britain.

Fortunately each of Wortley Hall's public rooms would be endowed by generous sponsors: the Foundry Workers, the Fire Brigades' Union, the Yorkshire Mineworkers, the Engineering Workers and the National Assembly of Women.

One of the rooms is the Sylvia Pankhurst Library, named after the famous socialist, suffragette and campaigner for women's rights. In conjunction with the National Assembly of Women a Sylvia Pankhurst lecture is held in the Library each year – delivered in 2006 by Sylvia Pankhurst's daughter-in-law Rita Pankhurst.

The Hague Wing commemorates the name of the first Secretary and his family. Each of the Hall's bedroom wings is named after Labour movement leaders: Keir Hardie, Harry Johnson, George Lansbury, Tom Mann, Abe Moffatt, Robert Owen, and, most importantly, Vin Williams.

Vin Williams, the founder of 'Labour's Home' was born in the Sheffield suburb of Woodhouse. He entered the pits at the age of 13: by the time of the General Strike of 1926 he was also a part-time organiser for the Labour Party.

During the General Strike Williams organised a strike bulletin, 'The Derbyshire Chronicle', and as a result was charged with committing an act calculated to cause mutinous sedition and sentenced to two months imprisonment with hard labour, plus a £5 fine.

Vin Williams had been sacked from his job for his political and trade union activity by the late 1940s and had taken up part-time lecturing for the National Council of Labour Colleges. He ended his working life as a full-time organiser with the National Council of Labour Colleges, lecturing and organising meetings relating to working-class politics.

In 1949 Vin Williams heard that Wortley Hall was empty and on the market. He immediately began making enquiries since, for a number of years, he had believed that the working class should own such a building for use as an education and holiday centre.

Effective from September 1950 the rent would be £50 for the first year, and £500 a year thereafter, with a lease period of 14 years.

When in June 1950 a national appeal was launched to raise the necessary money to

*Top: A Classic car show taking place in the grounds of Wortley Hall. **Above left:** Each year in conjunction with the National Assembly of Women, the Sylvia Pankhurst lecture is held, in 2006 it was delivered by Rita Pankhurst, pictured right, also pictured are Rita's husband Richard Pankhurst and Barbara Switzer, President of the National Assembly of Women. **Left:** Ukranian Dancers at the South Yorkshire Festival, 1995.*

convert Wortley Hall into an educational holiday centre a total of £1,300 was originally pledged.

Surveyors, brought in to advise on the cost of renovation and conversion, estimated that up to £50,000 would have to be spent. A further appeal was launched in local workplaces, factories, pits and building sites. Volunteers from amongst all trades, professions and housewives came forward to freely offer their services.

From September 1950 to May the following year the Hall was a beehive of activity as the volunteers poured in cleaning, renovating and converting the Hall and its grounds. To gain some measure of the amount of voluntary labour given to Wortley Hall the actual cost of converting, furnishing and fitting out the Hall was only £10,000.

Wortley Hall, now officially 'Wortley Hall (Labour's Home)', was formally opened by Sir Frank Soskice QC MP on 5th May 1951 in front of some 3,000 supporters.

With the death of the Earl in 1954 the entailment conditions attached to the property became null and void, and in order to help meet death duties the estate was now willing to sell the Hall.

Together with six cottages and approximately 28 acres of land, the Hall would change hands for just £10,000. On 28th October 1959 Wortley Hall (Labour's Home) finally took over the legal freehold.

Wortley Hall has come a long way since the 1950s. Then, still recovering from the war years, many people were easily satisfied and were prepared to sleep in dormitory bedrooms and gather around a coal fire in the evenings. Today aspirations are higher. Successive elected officers have striven to ensure that Wortley Hall continues a policy of progress by providing bedrooms with en-suite facilities, offering fully equipped conference training rooms, and providing a top quality service. Any operating surplus is spent on the Hall, either on maintenance or development, and on the well-earned profit sharing bonus scheme enjoyed by members of staff.

Still run on co-operative principles, the business has diversified from its original purpose of simply providing facilities for conferences and accommodation for holidays. In 1950 it was never envisaged that weddings would be held in the Hall, but today the Hall has a licence to hold

Above: Actor, Martin Clunes during the filming of "A" is for Acid, the story of serial killer John Hague. *Below left:* Fire Brigades Union - Black, Ethnic and Minority (BEAM) Annual School 2000. *Below:* The new lecture room named after former President Stewart Charnley is opened by his wife Betty, alongside Betty is Andy Gilchrist the General Secretary of the Fire Brigades Union.

Sadly in March 2004 Stewart Charnley who had been President since 1996 passed away. A much –respected member and Vice President of the Fire Brigades Union, he had been involved with Wortley Hall for many years. A new lecture room was named after him in 2005.

Change and improvements continue apace. Also in 2005 some 10,000 separate pieces of glass in the celebrated ceiling of the Foundry Dining Room were cleaned and renovated at a cost of over £40,000, half of which was met by donations from organisations and individuals. That same year the magnificent wood-paneled Board Room (previously the Lady Wharncliffe Sitting Room) was totally renovated and equipped with state of the art IT equipment and video conferencing facilities – all funded by the trade union Amicus.

Early in 2006 Amicus, successor to the AEU, also funded the redecoration and recarpeting of the AEU Lounge which the AEU had 'adopted' in the 1950s.

civic wedding ceremonies which have proved highly popular. Today an annual highlight is the South Yorkshire Festival held on the first Saturday in July (International Co-operators Day), a family festival celebrating different aspects of the Labour, Trade Union and Co-operative movements that brings the many supporters of Wortley Hall together.

In 2006 the theme of the festival was the 70th anniversary of the outbreak of the Spanish Civil War. An olive tree was planted to mark the occasion. Guest speaker was Jack Jones who fought in Spain with International Brigade before later becoming General Secretary of the Transport and General Workers Union.

Wortley Hall goes from strength to strength with its special relationship with trades unions, Labour Party branches and the Co-operative movement continuing in harmony with its mission statement:

'Our place in the Labour Movement history will be continually strengthened by our ability to anticipate the requirements of our customers and provide a quality of service which exceeds their expectations.'

The story of Wortley Hall though does not end here. Achieving and exceeding the vision of those early pioneers is still the objective of its officers.

Today those connected with Wortley Hall are justifiably proud of all the work done, and still being done, to continue the dream of Wortley Hall's past supporters. The founders' vision is shared with today's supporters who remain ambitious to go even further.

Above all the story of Wortley Hall over the last half-century has been one of true socialism in action. When

one recalls who built Wortley Hall in the first instance it can honestly be said that there is at least one place in Britain where the wheel of social change has made a full turn.

Top left: *The new AEU Lounge after redecoration and carpeting.* **Above:** *Jack Jones.* **Above right:** *The new Stained Glass windows. At a cost of £43,573 the work entailed replacing over 10,000 separate pieces of glass.* **Right:** *The newly renovated panelled Boardroom.*

Sheffield Testing Laboratories - Testing Times

Sheffield Testing Laboratories Ltd. (STL) based in Nursery Street is one of the UK's leading independent companies specialising in testing and calibration. The firm began trading in 1880.

The enterprise was begun by Thomas Nash. Born in Swindon, Nash settled in Sheffield where he became an inspector of railway rolling stock.

A steel tester and consulting engineer, Nash had offices in Fitzallan Square and Norfolk Street. By 1893 the business was known as the Sheffield Testing & Experimental Works. By 1898 it was based in Blonk Street where it would remain for over 60 years.

In the 1890s 'STEW' was undertaking a wide range of work 'testing for iron, metal, steel, steel and hemp ropes.'

Much of STEW's early growth was on the back of railway boom, which had spread to South America financed by British capital.

In February 1903 the Experimental was dropped and 'STW' was registered as a limited company. Later that same month however, Thomas Nash died. His son William RT Nash took over as managing director, but his early death in 1910 severed the family's direct link with the firm though his widow remained a shareholder.

The firm was run until the 1920s by the two Livesey brothers James and Sir Fernando Livesey, consulting engineers who had been directors at the time of the founder's death.

Regular customers included: Associated Portland Cement, John Brown, Cammell Laird and the Cunard Steamship Company, Daniel Doncaster, Ebbw Vale Iron & Steel, Samuel Fox, Vickers Sons and Maxim. In addition, thanks to a European tour by works manager William Cleland continental clients were also on the customer list.

Tests both small and large were carried out for as little as 1s 6d (7 1/2p) and up to five guineas (£5.25) for more complex work.

The highest paid workers earning just £2 9 shillings (£2.45) for a 52 hour week. Leonard Evans, who later became the company's technical director, was then receiving just 5 shillings (25p) a week as an apprentice.

The number of employees grew, the workforce expanding from 24 in 1905 to 36 in 1914 on the eve of the Great War.

The period 1914-18 saw a concentration on war work. Not least there was a large expansion in the amount of aeronautical inspection.

STW employees demonstrated their patriotism by volunteering to join up. A Roll of Honour produced by the company featured the names and photographs of eight employees who enlisted in the early months of the war. These eight volunteers received a promise of re-engagement on their discharge from the works manager William Cleland.

By late 1918 the workforce had more than doubled from pre-war levels to reach 106. This number included two women who were the first females other than the 'charwoman' to be employed.

The end of the war saw the workforce falling back to just 39.

In the 1920s STW directors included the famous steel-making names of Henry Steel and Albert Peech of Steel, Peech & Tozer fame. The United Steel Company held over 6,000 shares. Messrs Sandberg, a London firm of consulting and inspecting engineers undertook the management and control on behalf of United Steel, with three members of the Sandberg family joining the board in 1923. The same year William Cleland who had been with the firm since its early days, first as superintendent and later as works manager, became general manager, a role he occupied until his death in 1934.

During the inter-war years the company continued testing for railways. The company had its own resident inspector who from the 1930s was Ernest Moss. STW also had inspecting engineers in Cardiff and Manchester -and one in Belgium, CW Hatt, through whom the company secured a lot of work from South America.

Much of the work was straightforward mechanical testing, but analyses of such materials as wire rope could often be

Top left: An early 20 century view of The Sheffield Testing & Experimenting Works.
*Left: William Cleland. **Below:** A cheque paid to Sheffield Testing Works by Cooper & Turner for the amount of one pound and seventeen shillings, July 1922.*

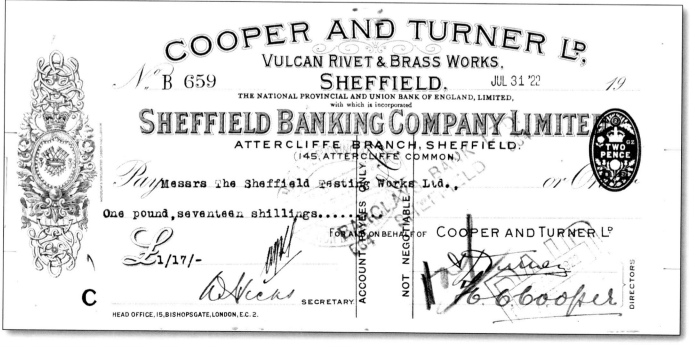

much more complicated, sometimes taking up to ten days. Testing charges were still relatively low with a number of tests still costing as little as 5 shillings (25p) at the start of the 1930s.

A new departure by STW was the start of production of 'proving rings', devices mainly for the calibration of the force-indicating mechanism of tensile testing machines, as well as for measuring tension loads and testing concrete beams. The products depend on being able to manufacture steel rings of precise physical characteristics.

After the death of William Cleland, George Westlake Vickers took over as general manager in 1935. He had been apprenticed to Cleland and later held an executive post in the company. An Old Harrovian he was remembered as 'A pretty severe but fair man' by former employee Charles Salzman who joined STW in 1937 at the age of 14.

Charles Salzman retired in 1995; he had become chief clerk in 1967. He recalled the early days when the reporting office used very elaborate forms and issued certificates on bond paper emblazoned with a coat of arms and scrollwork. He recalled the back of the Blonk Street works being used as a fairground twice a year until 1940, with the owner of the fair arriving in a polished mahogany caravan. Other recollections include the joint outings held annually until 'riotous behaviour' on a Pullman on the way back from London led to separate works and office trips.

The second world war again boosted employee numbers. War work included Bailey Bridge testing. One of the other main activities was machining small valves used in ships and aircraft. Women were again brought into the works, this time permanently. Other memories of those days come from John Walker who became the firm's technical director in 1973 and then managing director before his retirement in 1997. Recruited in 1942 at the age of 14 by the company secretary Dickie Dyke who

Top: A company letterhead from 1943.
Right: Dr W G 'Billy' Ibberson who joined the board in 1960 and succeeded George Vickers as chairman in 1967. Facing page: Installation of a 'new' 50tonne testing machine in the 1920's.

visited local schools to enlist 'likely lads'. John became an apprentice on the tensile test bench; he began work at 7.15am only finishing at 8pm on Tuesdays and Thursdays – not to mention working Saturday mornings too. One perk of the job was collecting faulty drills thrown into the river Don from the Osborn Works opposite and selling them for scrap.

After the war, led by chairman Howard Meredith Hardy, there was a change in the type of business. A house-building boom now led to a lot of construction material testing work. There was also a considerable amount of work from the newly-formed National Coal Board

Steel nationalisation led the United Steel Company to sell its stake in STW in 1951 enabling departmental managers to take small shareholdings for the first time.

By 1958 turnover had reached a record level of £54,000: rearmament at the time of the Korean War had helped stimulate business.

The early 1960s saw many changes. In 1960 local industrialist William 'Billy' Ibberson, head of the Sheffield cutlery firm George Ibberson joined the board. The following year STW lost its managing director with the death of AJW Graham who had held the post since 1941. The firm's general manager George Vickers was appointed to take his place.

Other important developments took place in 1963 when two long-serving members of staff, Cyril Atkins, the chief chemist, and Leonard Evans, its engineer, were appointed to the board. This was the first time that board members had been chosen 'from the ranks'. Leonard Evans had a national reputation in his field and used to lecture at Sheffield University; as early as 1927 he had presented a paper at the Institution of Engineering Inspection in London on stress-strain and the testing of rolling stock draw gear.

After seven decades at Blonk Street compulsory purchase forced STW to move to purpose-built premises in Nursery Street in 1962. The famous Sheffield firm of Thomas Ward laid special foundations including cork lining twelve inches thick to cushion the reverberating shock from the 200 tonne testing machine.

At the front of the works was the investigations department which examined why specimens failed in use and also had its own machine shop for preparing test specimens. The mechanical testing department featured not only the 200 tonne hydraulic testing machine but also a 50 tonne and 3,000kg machine for smaller items, as well as a special machine for tensile and compression testing of welds. The department also included other more specialised equipment for such things as impact and fatigue testing and for determining maximum crushing stress of concrete.

The chemical laboratory which continued to put the emphasis on the reference 'wet' chemistry approach had a large 8 bay fume cupboard as its central feature as well as extensive preparation and apparatus rooms which could offer salt spray and many other forms of testing, including equipment for testing flashpoints, calorific values, and testing oils.

Over the years STW had gradually extended its range of tests and chemical analyses until by this date it was offering a wide variety of physical tests for materials ranging from special alloys and Titanium, building materials and cement right through to tools and wire ropes. Chemical analyses were undertaken for everything from ferrous and non-ferrous metals and alloys to rubber, tar and varnishes.

The firm however suffered a blow in 1965 with the death of managing director George Vickers. Then over 80 years old he had been one of the company's longest-serving executives having become general manager in 1935. STW was however fortunate when Billy Ibberson became chairman in 1967. A true 'Sheffield Blade' Billy Ibberson was a former Master Cutler and past president of the Sheffield Chamber of Commerce; he was also one of the

founders of the Cutlery and Allied Trades Research Association.

Another change occurred in 1976 when Paul Fox, an expert in non-destructive testing, was appointed to the board. He became managing director in 1983 and subsequently chairman.

STW continued to develop its testing facilities. Around 1980, after undergoing months of rigorous testing the company secured the award from the Ministry of Defence of the coveted certificate of accreditation MOD 05-32 together with accreditation by the newly formed National Testing Laboratory Accreditation Scheme (NATLAS) for a range of testing operations and chemical analyses.

Another important advance came in 1984 with the opening of a department of 'force calibration' and 'dimensional metrology' for the calibration of precision instruments. The following year the 'Calibration Department' was accredited by the British Calibration Service (BCS).

Subsequently NATLAS and BCS joined to become NAMAS and latterly the United Kingdom Accreditation Service (UKAS).

With the retirement in 1984 of Heber Goodinson who had been with STW for 50 years as director and company secretary Wallace Hible became the new company secretary. Two year later ME Fox and John Walker joined the board.

In 1988 the company changed its name to Sheffield Testing Laboratories to more accurately reflect the fact that the enterprise was becoming increasingly scientific.

During 1994 the mechanical test house was moved to the front of the building and the machine shop to the rear where the loading and lifting facilities were located. Simultaneously machining and testing facilities were upgraded and computerised. Also at this time John Walker was made Managing Director and David Tame, the present General Manager, was appointed.

STL was acquired in 1996 by Cortest Laboratories a private UK company specialising in corrosion and corrosion testing. Cortest's chairman Dr John Oldfield would become chairman of both firms.
In 1998 the building 'next door' at 50-52 Nursery Street was purchased by the company, that same year the Cortest Laboratory trading was 'hived down' into STL.

The building purchase, almost doubled the space available to 40,000 square feet. This allowed the development of purpose built corrosion laboratories that included an electrochemical laboratory, an autoclave high temperature high pressure testing room and a dedicated laboratory for testing in hydrogen sulphide environments. These new facilities allowed the expansion of the corrosion testing business, particularly for the Oil and Gas industry. In addition a library was established, a boardroom, a meeting/training room, a canteen and a staff gym.

Incorporating the Cortest trading into STL meant that the entire operation could be run more smoothly, with the added benefit of cost savings. As a result Cortest Laboratories became the holding company for Sheffield Testing Laboratories.

The Company now operates with three Divisions, Mechanical Testing, Material Testing and Calibration. The Mechanical Testing Division uses state of the art equipment which can test up to 2000kN; test procedures can be tailored to best suit customers' needs. Testing is supported by a modern machine shop, which has CNC machining facilities and heat treatment capabilities.

The Material Testing Division offers a comprehensive range of material testing and consultancy services. The Division has well- equipped chemical analysis, corrosion and metallurgical laboratories.

The Calibration Division offers the calibration and repair of an extensive range of measuring instruments and gauges for force, torque, dimensional and pressure applications.

Sheffield Testing Laboratories have certainly come a long way since the business was founded back in 1880.

Top left: *from left to right: Former owner Paul Fox raises a glass with new owners Allen Denzine and Dr John Oldfield.* ***Below:*** *In 2000 Dr John Oldfield welcomed Lord Sainsbury to view the latest technology at Sheffield Testing Laboratories.*

Arkote - A Cut Above

Arkote Ltd is based in the heart of Sheffield – a city famous for the production of quality steel products for centuries. Over the past century the company has evolved to become one of the world's leading suppliers of knives to the tobacco industry alongside a range of other products and services.

Today Arkote continues to work with the leading machine manufacturers to develop knives which will give greater cutting efficiency and long life at reasonable cost.

The differing applications encountered throughout the tobacco industry have given Arkote the skill and experience to recommend exactly the knives most suitable for every type of cutting situation.

With greater demand for increased production down the decades has come the need for consistent high quality and reduced downtime. Arkote has had the skill and the reputation to rise to that challenge and to produce knives capable of exceptionally high performance and long life.

Arkote Limited took its name from a contraction of the name of its parent firm: AR Heathcote & Company. The original business was formed by Albert Reaney Heathcote in 1881 and at the outset operated from Dacre Street in the Park

district of Sheffield which is where the Parkhill flats would later stand.

Born in the first decade of Queen Victoria's reign, company founder, AR Heathcote, had previously been a chisel and edge tool manufacturer. The first sale of tobacco knives by him was recorded on 5th April 1881 to WD & HO Wills for the sum of £24 17 shillings. From that time on the firm would continue to supply specialist knives to makers of tobacco cutting machines.

But such knives were not the only product. At the same time the company was also selling edge tools and in addition had a flourishing business in grindstones quarried at Ackworth near Pontefract.

Though the business prospered until the first world war, it then declined as its founder grew older and the worldwide economic slump of the 1920s and 1930s arrived to crush many businesses out of existence.

In August 1919 AR Heathcote, then aged 75, took Percy F Osborne into partnership and a limited company was formed. Mr Heathcote was now Chairman and Mr Osborne, who had previously been works manager for J Riley Carr, was Managing Director. Following Mr Heathcote's death in 1941 at the remarkable age of 97, Mr Osborne became the sole owner of the company and assumed the Chairmanship.

During the period between the two world wars the company's activities had undergone a significant change. The edge tool business had disappeared and now the main activity was the manufacture of knives for the tobacco industry. The company had extended its activities into the manufacture of machine knives for the paper, metal-working and woodworking industries.

A new factory had been opened in Sydney Street, Sylvester Gardens in March 1934. P Sidney Osborne joined the company in the same year, followed by John Osborne in 1939.

In the course of the second world war the products of the company were essential to the war effort: in addition to knives the company also manufactured Primer Cap Plates (PCPs) which were used in the manufacture of percussion caps, and tank turret doors which were supplied to Vauxhall Motors.

After the war the company continued to expand and diversify. The demand for its products was such that by 1950 it had become necessary to acquire more manufacturing space. In the meantime there had been a revolutionary change in the method of cutting tobacco: this involved a totally different type of knife being used which in turn meant the need for new machinery and new methods of production.

*Top left: P F Osborne, known to all as Percy, father of John Osborne. **Left:** Samuel Staniforth's circa 1900. **Below:** Sydney Osborne, John Osborne and Joe Truelove.*

As a consequence in June 1950 Arkote was formed. It began operation in Hope Valley and continued there until 1955.

Production was moved back to Sheffield when it was difficult to recruit local labour. There Arkote produced the modern types of tobacco cutting knives which were still marketed under the old and respected name of Heathcote, although since the inauguration of Arkote the sale of its products to certain customers had been made on a direct basis.

Percy F Osborne sadly died in November 1961. Sidney Osborne succeeded him as Chairman of AR Heathcote Ltd whilst John Osborne became Chairman and Managing Director of Arkote Ltd.

It had been decided by then to consolidate production and sales by concentrating all activities connected with the tobacco industry at Arkote whilst AR Heathcote took over all the companies' other products.

Arkote finally moved into its present premises at Hawk Works, Mary Street in January 1962 where it operated as an entirely separate entity from AR Heathcote under the direction of John Osborne and Percy Osborne's grandson Joe Truelove.

In 1969 AR Heathcote & Company was sold to Balfour Darwins Limited, after which it had various owners as the Sheffield steel industry was reorganised: it finally ceased manufacturing several years ago.

Arkote however had a different future in front of it. In 1979 Arkote purchased Samuel Staniforth Limited a very old-established Sheffield cutlery forge, and although the forge was closed some years ago the company would for two decades become one of the main manufacturers of trade knives used in the catering and meat industries. This business was sold by Arkote in 1999.

In the meantime after a very serious fire at the Hawk Works in 1985 the efforts made by the whole workforce at Arkote to get production restarted illustrates the wonderful corporate spirit of the whole concern. No customers were let down, and indeed very few were even aware how close Arkote had been to disaster. Many of the staff have very long service records and it has been said 'Arkote workers don't leave they retire'.

In 2002 Chairman John Osborne and Managing Director Joe Truelove took the decision to sell the business and in December 2002 the company was bought by Fi-Tech Inc of Richmond Virginia in the USA. Not everything however would change: John Osborne remains a Director of the company.

Fi-Tech inc. is owned by the Bassett family; the company had been the distributor for Arkote products in the USA and Canada since 1980, although its Chairman Lee Bassett

cigar cutting knives and a re-grinding service for cork cutters.

Arkote is also able to supply a complimentary range of knife grinding products used both in the primary and making/tipping areas of a tobacco manufacturing facility.

High quality bonded abrasive wheels made to original manufacturers' specifications can be supplied for most model tobacco cutters. The Diamond Dressers required to dress these wheels are also supplied by Arkote.

had been involved with the distribution of Arkote products since 1967.

The Fi-Tech company is the supplier of a well known range of Adamantine Grinding Wheels and Discs, first introduced to the tobacco industry in 1967. These electroplated abrasive tools made to original manufacturers' specifications are utilised in all cigarette makers and tippers, and contain either high quality industrial diamond or Borazon®, a synthetic diamond material manufactured by the General Electric Corporation in the USA. A modern and environmentally-friendly process is used to manufacture these wheels and discs.

Meanwhile back in Sheffield close links with special steel technology and the ability to implement new advances in the manufacturing programme have been the key factors in the continuing success of the Arkote range of knives.

Yet although the most modern techniques play an important part in the Arkote production programme, the eye and the hand of the craftsman remain vital in determining the quality of the finished product.

The present factory, utilising rolled alloy steel and having continuous electric furnaces and automatic grinding and polishing equipment is a far cry from the early production methods. Strict quality control throughout all processes ensures consistency in size, temper and finish, so that Arkote products are recognised everywhere for their trouble-free performance and built-in efficiency.

As well as producing knives for primary and secondary cigarette production, the company also offers a range of

Arkote is a world leader in its niche market and exports up to 90 per cent of its production to over 80 countries all over the world. To complement its high quality products Arkote also provides a prompt and reliable delivery service to any part of the world.

There are now plans to relocate to a new purpose built factory to facilitate expansion and production improvements. With its origins in the 19th century, Arkote today is thriving in the 21st.

Left: *Arkote's heat treatment Department.*
Above: *The automatic polishing department.*
Below: *Arkote's Directors 2007 ; John Osborne, Peter Skinner - Managing Director, Lee Bassett – Chairman, Jeff Bassett.*

Fletchers - Baked to Perfection

On 16th July 2006 housewives in Sheffield could be forgiven for imagining that they had left their cakes in their ovens a little too long. The source of the smoke however was not to be found in household kitchens but at Fletchers Bakeries in Claywheels Lane. The fire was so large that smoke could be seen all across Sheffield.

Some parts of the Fletchers site were utterly destroyed. Yet, phoenix-like, new plant and equipment has been rising from the ashes of the old - the fire providing the impetus for even greater investment in modern technology.

Fletchers Bakeries bakes millions of products every week, making Claywheels Lane one of the leading bakeries in Britain – but where did it come from?

Small corner shop bakers were the dominating force in bread making until the second world war, but major changes in production capacity meant they would be progressively challenged by larger commercial bakeries operating on an

industrial scale. And one firm which would keep pace with those changing trends would be Fletchers.

Company founder, George Henry Fletcher, was not a Sheffield man, having been born in Horncastle in 1878. He began his working life as a farm labourer, later becoming a baker at Osier's Mill which ground its own corn and then used its own flour in its bakery. Since flour came in 15 stone sacks, bakers needed strong backs!

Together with his wife Kate, George Fletcher suffered many misfortunes as they tried to raise a family. Their poverty drove George to become an active member of the Bakers' Union and join enthusiastically in their fight for a

Above: Three generations of the Fletcher family George, George Henry, and Paul, pictured in the 1950s. Below: George Fletcher (right) and van boy Ernest Thompson stood infront of their Model T Ford. Right: Fletcher's Middlewood bakery opened in 1923.

60-hour week. Because of his union activities, he was blacklisted by employers and had no choice but to set up in business on his own. Having no capital, he began by baking just for local households.

Lack of money was not the only difficulty: a shortage of imported flour during the first world war meant queues outside the bakery. Even so, Fletchers had their first mechanical aid, an Artofex dough mixer installed in 1915 and soon afterwards acquired a Model T Ford for deliveries.

In the meantime George was becoming something of a local hero from his championing of workers' rights and his business efforts were supported by them; so much so that by 1923 he was able to open a new bakery in the reasonably prosperous area of Middlewood Road, Hillsborough. He was determined to run his business on egalitarian principles and to improve the conditions within the bakery industry as a whole.

George's son, George junior, who had little luck in his career as a mechanic, joined his father and the two men took the bread they had baked out on a barrow to sell on the street. The poor flocked to buy from them and business flourished.

Fletchers' sixth bakery opened in Penistone Road in 1926 . It was

equipped with a two-deck Baker Perkins oven, revolutionary progress for those times. By 1936, there were 11 large red vans. With George junior's engineering background, every machine in every bakery became his concern.

During the second world war, following the second Sheffield blitz, there was a bakery fire – though due to an employee's error rather than the Luftwaffe. George was undismayed, laconically commenting 'it was about time we had a clear out'. It was the spirit in which he conducted the business until his death in 1958 at the age of 79.

Claywheels Lane would become the site of the firm's seventh bakery. George junior noticed this ideal site when he took his son Paul sledging in Wadsley Bridge; he bought the site in 1947.

In 1950 production began, and for many years the business flourished. However, in the 1970s, demand for bread fell. A discount war began, but the company resisted take-over bids from larger bakeries. Sliced bread was in demand but bagging-machines for it caused Fletchers more problems than any other piece of machinery. Even worse, entry into the Common

Above: The firms's fleet pictured in 1936.
Left: Fletchers' Claywheels Lane works.

Market increased the price of flour because of punitive levies on North American wheat. Fletchers, however, retained 50 per cent of Canadian wheat in their flour and continued making 'open' confectionery when other firms resorted to pre-packed.

Following the death of George Fletcher junior in 1973 the business passed to his son Paul. George had been an inspired engineer at a time when technology was the key to advancement. Paul's talents were organisational; he took an overall look at the bakery and kept an eye on what was happening in the baking world outside, picking up the best ideas and innovations. As a result Fletchers became the first bakers in Europe to introduce a 'Lanham' plant. The new equipment cost £500,000 but could produce 14,000 burger buns in an hour; automation now gradually took over most of the processes. Freezer plants were introduced in 1983; now the company could sell nationwide.

By 1991, Fletchers was offering an extensive range of fresh and frozen foods, producing millions of doughnuts, scones and burger buns each week. Sadly, the 1990s brought with them the decision to close all Fletchers' high street shops, including the flagship outlet in Exchange Street. Meanwhile, baking staff continued to

be treated as well as they had been by the company founder, being amongst the best paid in the industry.

Today, Fletchers only rarely sell its products direct to the consumer; the business is now split into two main parts: 'Foodservice' where Fletchers' products are sold to the catering industry wholesalers, some of whom resell them under their own labels, and 'Retail' where the same range of products goes to major multiples, which also sell mainly under their own labels.

Top left: Mammoth Muffins - Fletchers' Taste of America.
Above: One of the firm's state-of-the-art ovens.
Below: Fletchers' distinctive new livery.

The core product range is supplied in retailer own label to the likes of Tesco, Sainsbury's and Marks & Spencer's and you may even find yourself enjoying a scone or muffin in your favourite café!

La Baguette Doree (LBD) became part of group in November 2005. This factory in Barnsley produces high quality bread products, including many hand-finished and organic items and is an exciting addition to the capabilities of the Fletchers group.

At the turn of the millennium Paul Fletcher retired. After being a family-owned firm for almost the whole of the 20th century, in 1999 Fletchers was taken over by Northern Foods, one of the country's leading food producers, which could now supply Fletchers with more resources, knowledge and support. The Fletchers' name however remained, far from disappearing a new Fletchers' group emerged, made up of Fletchers in Sheffield, Kara in Manchester and Grain D'Or in London, with the group head office based in Sheffield.

In early 2007 the Fletchers Group ownership changed hands once again and now forms part of the Eliot Group of food companies.

Plans for further development of the Fletchers business continue with investment in new and improved manufacturing capability at the top of the list just as it always was under the family ownership over the last 100 years. Further information can be found on the company's website: www.fletchersbakeries.co.uk.

Top left: HRH Prince Andrew, visits the Fletchers stand at the International Food Expo. *Centre:* A selection of Fletchers' high quality bread products. *Below:* Fire tears through the bakery in 2006.

Fletchers now have no fewer than 16 producing units, making both fresh and frozen products, with a capacity to bake more than 25 million items every week and a turnover of a hundred million pounds each year.

Fletchers is the UK's largest producer of muffins with two production plants in Sheffield and two further plants in London. In addition it's a major supplier of bread, rolls, French bread, scones and doughnuts.

Outokumpu - A stainless past, a spotless future

Sheffield, the heart of Britain's special steel industry, is naturally a centre for stainless steel, but it is also the very city in which metallurgist Harry Brearley discovered this metal marvel.

Harry was born in Ramsden's Yard off Spital Street in 1871. Although having a difficult start in life, young Harry attended night school becoming a metallurgist and co-author of 'The Analysis of Steelworks Material' – one of the earliest key texts of the subject.

In 1913 Harry Brearley was examining the excessive wear of rifle barrels and wondered if a chromium steel might perform better. On 20th August 1913, Brearley supervised the making of a cast containing 12.8 per cent chromium and 0.24 per cent carbon.

Above: *Harry Brearley.*
Right: *An early stainless steel knife.*
Below: *Tinsley Roll mill's pictured in the 1900s.*

Ferrous metal which kept its shine was a dream. Before the First World War anything made of steel quickly rusted away if it wasn't kept polished and oiled.

The new alloy was extremely resistant to attack of all kinds. Ordinary steels react with oxygen and water in the atmosphere to form a hydrated iron oxide - rust - which, being porous, permits further oxidisation and rust. With stainless steel, however, the oxide formed is chromium oxide, quite different from rust. Although very thin, (equivalent to a single playing card placed on the top of a ten storey building), this impermeable layer protects the metals surface from any further reaction and, when scratched, reforms in seconds.

On the continent, others came up with another type of chromium alloy, this one containing nickel. Although the

continental alloy was too soft for knives, it was easier to shape.

In Sweden, the importance of the development was recognised by what was then the Avesta Jernwerks Company. It financed extensive research into stainless

steels and bought a license to manufacture them from the British. The first chromium alloy steel was produced in Sweden in 1924. The discovery opened up a massive commercial opportunity for rustproof cutlery.

Stainless steel has had an enormous impact in restaurants and domestic dining rooms. New compositions have developed for wide ranging applications such as low maintenance, long life cladding for commercial buildings; engineered surfaces for easy cleaning in the catering and food processing industries; as well as in surgical applications and in military hardware. Easily formed varieties of this wonder alloy are ideal for the production of complex-shaped components such as fuel tanks, whilst also being ideal for the manufacture of oil and gas platforms able to resist the very worst of the North Sea.

The rationalisation of Britain's steel industry saw the coming together of United Steel Companies Ltd, which, along with Firth Vickers, owned the rolling mills on Shepcote Lane, Sheffield. In 1974, the government announced a £130 million investment in facilities at Shepcote Lane, which included enhanced cold rolling and annealing and pickling capabilities. In 1977 the go ahead was also given to create a dedicated stainless steel melting shop – SMACC (Stainless Melting and Continuous Casting).

After the privatisation of BSC in 1988, British Steel Stainless was created as the dedicated stainless arm of British Steel. British Steel Stainless then joined forces with Avesta AB in 1992. This created Avesta Sheffield AB and a new company symbol – the European bison.

Below: An aerial view of the Trade Centre - the final legacy of British Steel Stainless. A massive investment was made to create the largest and most comprehensive dedicated stainless steel finishing facility in Europe.

The famous two-tonne hollow cast stainless steel bison, a replica of the Swedish original, was erected on Avesta Sheffield land adjacent to the M1 motorway in 1994.

In 2001 a merger between Outokumpu Steel and Avesta Sheffield created Avesta Polarit. Outokumpu's history dates back to 1910 when a substantial copper ore deposit was found in Finland.

In 2004 all companies were united under one brand – Outokumpu Stainless Ltd.

Sheffield and Outokumpu - An Integrated Partnership

1848 A small company named Samuel Fox & Co starts business in Sheffield as a precision mill.

1854 First recording of Cold Rolling by Samuel Fox & Co.

1874 Arthur Lee is the General Manager of Crown Steel & Wire mill. This now changes title to Arthur Lee & Sons.

1910 Outokumpu's history dates back to 1910 when a substantial copper ore deposit was found in Finland.

1913 Harry Brearley develops Stainless Steel.

1914 Arthur Lee & Sons purchase a 25-acre site to build the Meadowhall site.

1920 Razor blade strip is rolled for the first time in Stocksbridge.

1922 The first continuous rolling mill is installed in the country.

1967 Stocksbridge Works became part of the British Steel Corporation.

1977 SMACC was built as a major investment in Stainless Steel manufacturing in Sheffield by British Steel Corp.

1992 Avesta AB merges with British Steel Precision Strip and British Stainless Steel.

1999 Avesta Sheffield AB acquires Lee Strip in Meadowhall - Precision Strip now produces thin narrow cold stainless steel and carbon steel strip from both UK sites.

2001 January 22nd the merger between Outokumpu Steel and Avesta Sheffield is completed to create Avesta Polarit, one of the world's largest stainless steel producers.

2003/4 Outokumpu Stainless Distribution relocates from Oldbury to a state-of-the-art service centre in Sheffield - the largest single investment in a UK stainless service centre.

2004 All companies were united under one brand to become Outokumpu Stainless Ltd.

2005 ASR was granted a Queen's award for Enterprise in the International Trade Category.

2005 Outokumpu ceases the operation of its Coil Production Division (CPS) business unit in Sheffield.

2006/7 Investment in Outokumpu Stainless Distribution meant the relocation of its Blackburn Plate Service Centre facilities to Sheffield.

Stainless Steel Bison

Since the company was no longer known as Avesta Sheffield the Outokumpu Stainless company agreed to donate the bison to a local visitor attraction. The two tonne bison, made up of 16 separate stainless steel pieces, has now taken up a new high profile position, where it will be seen by the hundreds of thousands of visitors every year. The bison is a symbol of the status and reputation of Stainless Steel in Sheffield and how important and central stainless steel was, and in many ways is today, in terms of industry in Sheffield. It represents a legacy of a great industry in a renowned city.

Outokumpu Steel is Everywhere

Outokumpu operates worldwide. From remote parts of China to the busy cities of America you can find Outokumpu Steel, and in some cases steel that has been melted or cold rolled in Sheffield.

Outokumpu Today

There were many changes that occurred during the merger of Avesta Polarit with Outokumpu with four business units left in Sheffield today.

These are Outokumpu Stainless Distribution, Sheffield Special Strip, ASR and SMACC. There was a Coil Products Division in Sheffield when the merger took place but Outokumpu ceased its operations and closed the division down in 2005.

Outokumpu is now one of the largest manufacturers of stainless steel in the world and one of only four in Europe. A modern, forward thinking company it is widely recognised for innovation development and quality, and

Above: Avesta Sheffield's Stainless Steel Bison that once overlooked the M1 motorway.
Right: Outokumpu Steel on Jin Mao, a building in Shanghai, China.
Far right: Outokumpu Steel on the Blue Cross Building in Chicago, USA.

has the broadest product range in the market selling its output in over fifty countries across the globe.

The company's plants at Europa Link, Stocksbridge, Meadowhall and Stevenson Road, as well as in Finland, Sweden and the USA, produce a wide range of stainless steel products, together with a comprehensive range of fittings and flanges.

Outokumpu's main products are cold and hot rolled stainless steel coil, sheet and plate. Other products include precision strip, hot rolled plate, long products as well as tubes and fittings.

SSS

Sheffield Special Strip is one business unit in the Outokumpu Group and one of the largest manufacturers of high quality specialised strip, with the most refined and greatest variation of stainless steel in the Group.

This steel is used in a whole spectrum of applications - from everyday goods to highly sophisticated industrial equipment. Applications include Razor Blades, Scalpels, and Electronic Components such as parts for Mobile Phones, Automotive Parts, tools in the Construction industry, Filtration products and Texture Rolled Strip.

Sheffield Special Strip posseses an unparalleled knowledge of metals production and processing. The SSS knowledge has been passed on down a long line of expert workers and engineers in Sheffield. The business unit dates back to the 1850s with the start of Precision Strip Manufacture.

Outokumpu Stainless Distribution

Outokumpu Stainless Distribution, relocated from Oldbury in 2003/2004, is an integral part of the Outokumpu Group. The state of the art distribution centre is the direct sales centre in the UK for most of Outokumpu's European plants and fulfils customer orders for a wide variety of stainless products including cold rolled coil/sheet, hot rolled continuously produced plate/ coil, quarto plate, tubes and fittings.

Outokumpu's stainless steel service centre in Sheffield has benefited from substantial investment in recent years and now enjoys state of the art processing, packaging and polishing equipment.

Most recently in 2006/2007 has been the relocation of the Blackburn Plate Service Centre to Outokumpu Stainless Distribution in Sheffield.

SMACC

SMACC (Stainless Melting and Continuous Casting) is the only dedicated stainless steel melting shop left in the UK today. Commissioned in 1977 it is one of three the Group possesses with another in Finland and one in Sweden.

The Sheffield melting shop has an annual capacity of approx 500,000 tonnes and supplies stainless steel semi finished products (including slabs, cast blooms and cast billets) to both internal and external customers worldwide.

SSS has greater flexibility to develop new product ranges and, with the Outokumpu factor, can make a real difference to clients' businesses and with access to a global sales force covering more than 60 countries from a network of offices that provide a locally-focused service.

The Business Unit manufactures stainless steel precision strip across the full spectrum of Austenitic, Martensitic, Texture Rolled Strip and Stainless Razor.

ASR

Also included in the Outokumpu Group is ASR Rod (Alloy Steel Rods) on Stevenson Road, Sheffield. ASR has decades of experience in producing stainless steel rod coil. Whilst being proud of its heritage, ASR Rod Mill is committed to looking into the future and meeting the needs of its customers in today's demanding market.

ASR supplies rod coil in a comprehensive range of grades, sizes and shapes which are then purchased as feedstock for others to turn into a diverse range of products including wire, drawn bar and fasteners.

In 2005 ASR was granted a Queen's Award for Enterprise in the International Trade Category.

Sheffield has much to be proud of, but none of its products has done more to shape the modern world than stainless steel. Today, worldwide, the demand for stainless steel is growing more rapidly than for any other metal.

Through the Outokumpu Group the city of Sheffield is continuing to shape the world.

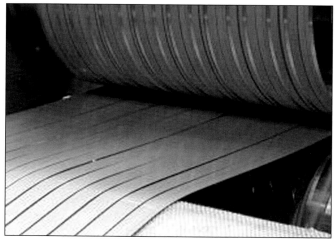

Top: *Coils of Bright Annealed material after cold rolling.*
Right: *The slitting of precision strip coils at SSS.*

Symmetry Medical - Thornton Precision Components
The Joint that Works

There are few firms that can definitely say that they make a real difference to people's lives. A few businesses however can claim to make profound differences to the quality of life for thousands upon thousands of folk – they are that small band of specialist firms involved in the manufacture and supply of modern medical miracles of technology.

In the 21st century it is possible to alleviate suffering in ways which were unimaginable to previous generations. Until the closing decades of the 20th century an old age, crippled with arthritis, was the inevitable price millions paid for living so long. The elderly expected to become housebound as their joints began to fail – a walking stick would give way to a walking frame and finally to a bed.

But miracles do happen: advances in medical techniques have meant that millions now get a second chance at an active life, long after their natural joints have given up the ghost.

Providing a single point of contact for all orthopaedic supply solutions Symmetry Medical – Thornton Precision Components (SMI-TPC) is a major player in the global orthopaedic market. Bought out by Symmetry Medical in June 2003, having previously been part of the Mettis Group, Thornton is now one of the world's largest manufacturer of artificial hip joints and a major supplier of cast femoral knee joints. Exporting around 70 per cent of its products, Thornton is a major supplier to the world's leading orthopaedic houses. Today the company, based in Beulah Road, has some 420 staff.

The firm of GW Thornton was established in 1895 by George William Thornton with the help of both his wife and brother. The business at that time was all about forging cutlery; it would grow to have some 350 employees.

The firm had begun in Lowther Road, but by the 1930s it had expanded, acquiring property not just in Beulah Road but also at Sedgely.

In those days press operators and 'stampers' - were surrounded by 'scale' from the metal pieces they worked with. The cutlery would arrive black and be buffed and polished till it shone. It was a dirty job.

Yet life at the firm it was not all dirt and work. Many will have memories of the works Sports Club, of trips to Blackpool, Skegness and Bridlington. Others will recall the Fishing Club, which still exists to this day.

A number of key people, still with the business, began work for the firm in the 1960s: Alan Pearson started as a straight rolling apprentice, has worked on the smallest stamp up to the 3 tonne stamp that was acquired in 1979.

Top left: George William Thornton.
Below: Early patent drawings.
Top right: An aerial view of the old GW Thornton Cutlery Forge and Cutlery Works site. *Below right:* Alan Pearson and Jim Thompson who between them have given the company 90 years of service.

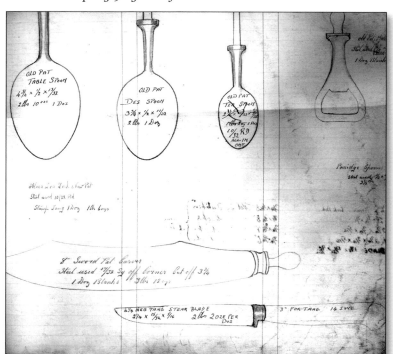

He is now the stamp shop manager. Jim Thompson, also now with 45 years of service, started on the pull stamps and would work every stamp up to the 3 tonne stamp. He now works in inspection and quality.

In the 1950s the company collaborated to develop implants, and in the 1960s instruments. During the early 1970s with the decline of the cutlery industry Thornton's began to use more challenging materials and manufacture more unusual items such as special alloys forgings for the aerospace industry.

Hip replacement with artificial joints was perfected by Sir John Charnley in Manchester in the 1960s. He found that joint surfaces could be replaced by first metal, and later high-density polyethylene, implants cemented to the bone.

In fact hip replacements had been first attempted towards the end of the 19th century, with gold and ivory being used to replace the femoral head, but it was in Manchester that Professor John Charnley made the real breakthrough with his famous 'Charnley Hip' which he had manufactured in Leeds.

Since then there have been continuous improvements in the design and technique of joint replacement. Amongst the contributors in the field was WH Harris whose team at Harvard in the USA pioneered uncemented techniques with the bone bonding directly to the implant. Further advances were made by Professor Muller from Switzerland and Professor Ling in Exeter.

Today in England alone over 55,000 primary (first time) hip replacements are now performed every year. The overall success of this major operation is 95 – 96 per cent. Knee replacements using similar technology to treat rheumatoid arthritis patients, and later sufferers from

osteoarthritis, began in the 1970s and have developed ever since.

With the continuing development of challenging materials during the early 1980s Thornton's pioneered the forging of cobalt chrome into orthopaedic implants, a material that is now widely used in the manufacture of orthopaedic products.

The early 1980s were marked by the arrival of two young men who would play an important part in the future of the firm.

Richard Senior arrived from the Engineering Industry Training Board after leaving school, on 30th June 1980. He started as an Inspector. He has since undertaken various roles, including Visual Inspector, Final Inspector, Sales Administration Manager, Sales Manager, Production Manager, Manufacturing Director, Operations Director, Director & General Manger and Managing Director. Today he is Senior Vice President of European Operations with overall responsibility for all of SMI's European operations.

Mark Corry arrived on 6th July 1981 at the age of 19, also coming from the Engineering Industry Training Board. Starting as a Trainee Press Operator he is now Managing Director of Thorntons.

The GW Thornton Group was bought out by the BI Group in 1995, which was keen to build upon the orthopaedic business and had an aggressive acquisition strategy, a strategy which also resulted in the acquisition of TG Lilleymans in Sheffield and the Jet Engineering company in the US creating the BI Engineering Division.

Top: Mark Corry, Managing Director of Thorntons (left) and Richard Senior, Senior Vice President of European Operations.
Right: Installation of the company's No.3 press in 1984.

The BI Engineering Group's domination of the orthopaedic forging market highlighted the fact that it had no presence in the market for orthopaedic castings. As a result the company invested over £4 million in 1998 building a dedicated orthopaedic casting facility based in Sheffield – making SMI the only company in the world with the ability to supply cast, machined or forged orthopaedic components.

That same year however, the company was sold by the BI Group via an Institutional Buy-Out, leading to the creation of the Mettis Group Ltd with its Head Office in Sheffield. From 1999 the Mettis Group invested heavily in its manufacturing facilities, particularly in the machining capabilities of SMI-TPC where cellular manufacturing of hips and knees now takes place following an investment of three quarters of a million pounds. The year 2000 TPC

saw an opportunity to supply femoral heads to the orthopaedics market – a market which until then had not been aggressively pursued. Dedicated machines requiring an investment of £750,000 were installed, which would see sales in that area increase by more than 130 per cent in three years.

In June 2003 the merger of Symmetry Medical and the Mettis Orthopaedics Group created a global orthopaedic supplier which could offer a comprehensive line of implants, surgical instruments and cases to the medical devices market throughout the world.

SMI-TPC Ltd Sheffield has become the European headquarters. To further grow the supply of its products SMI-TPC has invested even more in its femoral head manufacturing facility, spending £250,000 in plant and buildings, utilising production flow and an increase in capacity.

Additional investment has included £1.3 million in its femoral knee manufacturing cell to create capacity for new projects.

With changing world-wide demographics and changes in people's attitude towards health-

care – thanks to the baby boom generation and the rise of 'grey power' - the future looks prosperous for the whole of the orthopaedic market.

With an anticipated increase in demand in excess of 25 per cent annually SMI-TPC has placed itself strategically as a full service provider with a single point of contact for supplying Total Solutions for finished hip or finished knee systems.

To meet the anticipated increase in demand the company set out to complete a state of the art machining facility dedicated to orthopaedics by the end of 2004, with an overall investment of £6.2 million in plant and buildings.

With ever-increasing demand for its products and a willingness to invest in order to meet that demand Symmetry Medal – Thornton Precision Components has definitely left the word of cutlery behind it forever.

Above: Blade inspection.
Left: A small selection of Symmetry Medical products:
1, Custom spinal implants.
2, Knee components.
3 and 4, Symmetry Othy surgical instruments.
5, Hip components.

Dexel Tyre Company - Wheels of Progress

The invention of the pneumatic rubber tyre in the 19th century was one of the key developments contributing to the success of the motor vehicle industry in the 20th century.

Today, with millions of cars and commercial vehicles on the road, there is a huge demand for fuel, servicing, repair facilities – and of course new tyres.

In Sheffield the family-owed Dexel Tyre Co Ltd, with its headquarters in Staniforth Road, Attercliffe, is a name which has become synonymous with the tyre business.

The France family business really started in the early 1950s when they were in partnership with another family at Frecheville Garages Ltd. Prior to that venture Harry France had worked at what would later become Mushroom Garage (Rotherham) and his son Peter had worked at Globe and Simpson. Frecheville Garages was the main agent for Vulcan commercial vehicles, Austin cars and had a thriving vehicle repair and petrol forecourt business.

During 1955/56 the two families argued over workloads and shareholding, a disagreement which ultimately led to dissolution of the partnership and Frecheville

Garages eventually being put into voluntary liquidation in 1961.

In 1957 however the three France family shareholders at Frecheville Garages, Harry France, his wife Blanche and their son Peter, bought the land across the road from Frecheville Garages, and after securing a loan of £20,000 from the Regent Oil Company built a new petrol filling station on Birley Moor Road. Behind the petrol station was a Nissen hut from which they also began to sell tyres.

By 1959 the filling station was making a handsome return, and the tyre business was beginning to take off. On 10th November 1959 Dock Tyre Co Ltd was incorporated, it started trading in June 1960 from a leased property in Dock Road, Worksop.

The 1960s were busy times, and May 1960 witnessed the incorporation of the motor factoring business Autocom Units, a new company which filed its first trading accounts on 31st March 1961. The first trading premises of Autocom Units were situated next to Dock Tyres in Worksop.

Dexel Tyre Co Ltd was formed on 25th April 1961 and bought its first premises in Westbury Street from the

Above: *Harry France (right) and Peter France.*
Below: *The first Dock Tyre premises pictured in 1966.*
Right: *An early company van.*

now the manager at Dexel Frecheville and who has completed over 45 years service having joined the business in 1962.

Late in 1962 property was purchased in Bridge Street, Gainsborough and Dock Tyre and Autocom Units began trading there. That same year Dexel Tyre Co bought shares in Owlerton Green Garage and spread its business interests to North Sheffield.

Mrs Blanche Mary France died in 1963 and the whole shareholding in the firm now fell to the father and son combination of Harrry and Peter France. To further fuel expansion, which they were keen to do, a £20,000 debenture was secured with the Goodyear Rubber Company at the end of 1963. In 1964 the pair bought Highway Tyres in Great Central Road Mansfield, bringing the number of tyre outlets to five. Sadly due to pressure from the bank this very profitable business had to be sold to ATS in 1985.

liquidator of the old Frecheville Garages that same year. The sign on the Nissen hut at the far side of the Frecheville filling station now read Dexel and became the firm's first trading depot. By May that year Dexel on Westbury Street began trading supplying tyres for both cars and commercial vehicles.

Expansion would be rapid during the early 1960s, and 1962 saw the opening of Autocom Units in Sheffield. Not the least of those present at the opening was Peter Staton,

This page: *Interior and exterior views of Dexel in the late 1960s.*

In the early 1960s however the tyre side of the business continued to grow and in 1965 additional premises were found in Derby, however, the site never opened and was later sold. Owlerton Green Garage was also sold that year to raise funds to expand the tyre business. In 1965 land was bought on the opposite side of the road in Gainsborough so that a new purpose-built depot could be constructed for Dock Tyre.

In 1966 a new depot was opened on the old Intake Service Station site at the top of Woodhouse Road. Due to traffic congestion in this area however, the site never took off and was sold in 1979. Meanwhile 1966 had seen the opening of a new tyre car bay on Staniforth Road including a new reception and sales shop. Those there at the official opening included Keith Booth, another company stalwart who would still be with the firm more than 45 years later.

The site at Staniforth was quickly outgrown, and during the late 1960s many surrounding properties were acquired: a café and terraces next to Dexel were bought in 1968 and would subsequently become the truck

Right: Westbury Street, the site of the company's first premises pictured in the 1980s. **Below:** *Sheffield's Chief of Police cuts the ribbon at the official opening of Dexel's new car bay and reception on the Staniforth Road premises, 1966.*

department. Property in Selborne Street was acquired that same year for £1,665 and would later become the firm's battery store.

Further diversification came in 1968 when Peter convinced his father that there was a future in pickled onions. With a golfing friend Don Robinson they formed Central Foods based in Petre Street, Sheffield and traded as Mr Spicy Pickles. Things were also happening on the tyre side and land was acquired on Eastgate Worksop for a new depot for Dock Tyre. In this year the first petrol station on Birley Moor Road which had been the start of the family business was sold.

Expansion continued with the acquisition of Sayers Tyres in Doncaster in 1998 with sites at both ends of the town. Most recently, in 2000, City Tyre Experts of Lincoln was purchased with two depots in Lincoln and one in Market Rasen – a return to Market Rasen after some 25 years absence.

By 2005 Dexel was operating five separate limited companies all of them selling tyres and the task of separate administration was becoming very costly. A decision was therefore made to unite the whole group under the name of Dexel. Today Dexel has 11 depots all flying the Dexel flag, and a further two depots in Sheffield trading under the names of Mr Exhaust and One Stop.

The company now employs over 150 staff and has an annual turnover of £13 million made from selling 100,000 tyres every year.

In 2006 the fourth generation of the France family joined the company when James France, Paul's eldest son, started work at the Worksop branch, an event marking the start of the next era of the Dexel Group.

The year 2006 was also a time of celebration at Dexel when the France family were proud to honour 11 of their staff who between them had notched up no less than 364 years of service: the France family has certainly been doing something right!

Dock Gainsborough moved across the road in 1969 into purpose built property, and, with Dock having seen off the competition, Autocom moved into the old National Tyres depot further down the road at Chapel Staithe. Property was rented in Market Rasen for another Dock Tyre depot bringing the total to three. This last depot was however to prove short-lived as rising rents made it unprofitable: the depot would be closed in the mid-1970s.

The 1970s and 80s were a time of relative consolidation. Dock Tyres Worksop moved into new premises on Eastgate in 1973. Property was purchased in Horncastle and a fourth Dock Tyre depot was opened in 1972. Toolair, a repair business for the sale and repair of air tools was formed in the early 1970s.

The next generation of the France family entered the business in 1973 when Paul France the current Managing Director joined, followed by his sister Julie in 1983. Sadly 1980s saw the death of Harry France at the age of 75; exactly ten years later his son Peter died aged just 64.

Meanwhile the area around the head office in Attercliffe in the late 1970s was going through a major transformation as the streets of terraced houses were slowly cleared; even the old Langtons shoe factory was pulled down.

Under the direction of the next generation of the France family the business now started to move forward again. In 1990 part of the old Eagle Garage in Bradfield Road Hillsborough was purchased and Dexel Hillsborough was born.

In 1996, eager to increase their coverage in Sheffield, Dexel bought the very well known Mr Exhaust business with its two sites. These complimented the existing business and brought the number of tyre outlets to eight.

Top left: Raising a glass to the eleven employees of Dexel who between them have given the company 364 years of service. ***Below:*** *The France family, 2007, from left to right: Lesley, Paul, Doreen, James and Julie.*

Baker Blower - Excellence in Engineering

Mention the words turning, milling, honing, grinding and boring and anyone who has had any connection with industry knows exactly what we're talking about - engineering. From the earliest days of the steel industry the city of Sheffield has been home to highly skilled engineers keen to turn freshly cast metal into carefully-crafted metal components for steam engines and other complicated machines. Today the oil, gas and aerospace industries demand metal components made to even higher standards from Sheffield's famed engineers. And few names are more highly-regarded than that of Baker Blower.

The Baker Blower Engineering Company Ltd was founded by a man named Baker in 1873 and sold out to a partnership of Walter James Travis and a colleague named Sykes in 1937. The business was named after an air injection system for open-hearth furnaces which the firm came to specialize in. Baker Blower was born out of the Saville Street Foundry of Baker was an experienced and senior member of staff. He established the business in a house in Stanley Street shaded by a plant nursery.

Today the house is still there, the office building within Baker Blower's well known Special Works.

Until the late 1940s the company made over 100 Baker Blowers which were distributed throughout the United Kingdom and Europe. The last Baker Blower was made in 1950, but by that time the company had expanded into repair work and general machining. Much of that new work was a spin-off from the company's participation in the war effort when its employees had machined armour plating for tanks and made shell casings.

Walter Travis' grandson, Walter Harryman-Travis, eventually took over the firm. Baker Blower was by this time a limited company, and under his direction the firm survived the dramatic collapse of Sheffield's steel industry in the 1970s by developing the company's skills and adopting a more sophisticated approach to its stock trade.

Helpfully by the late 1970s the company had become 'Rolls-Royce Approved', a status enhanced in the 1980s by also gaining Rolls-Royce's 'Critical Part Approval'.

Yet despite the company's continuously improving reputation some rocky years would still lie ahead. From 1989 to 1994 traditional markets began to change, with some old ones disappearing altogether as economic recession hit.

Above: An early view inside the works. *Left:* An inspector looking at various types of rolls used in different industries.

in the industry, orders began to be received from the USA, France and Scotland.

Steve Hill' appointment as Works Manager in 1996 completed a very solid management team, which would be enhanced by Leigh Ashton who joined the company in 1997 and spearheaded a move into computerized accounts. By then the rest of the team would include Colin Hutson, Quality Manager, Chief Inspector Geoff Freeman and secretary Lorraine Rastall. Steve Hill would move from being Works Manager to become Production Director in 2002.

Since then the policy of investment has continued. New machinery allows work on super alloy materials; the latest CAD programs (Solid Works) and equipment are now being utilised, and enhanced quality systems introduced to meet the requirements of new aerospace, oil & gas customers.

Now able to take on contracts not previously possible, a new hi-tech customer base has been established as a result of investment. The direct result has been an increase in turnover and profits of 18%, and secure company prospects for six years or more.

Baker Blower has become one of the country's leading manufacturers of precision machined parts; its managers together with the highly skilled workforce are ready to meet the ever changing demands of the manufacturing world, bringing new business to Sheffield and proudly sending precision-engineered parts marked 'Made in Sheffield' all across the world.

Martin Birch, who was appointed Managing Director in 1994, revitalized the company; he restructured the machine shop, launched his 'Big Marketing Drive', introduced new quality systems helping the company gain the prestigious quality accreditation ISO9001 whilst simultaneously improving production and starting an apprenticeship scheme. Nor was that all: big investments were now made in computer aided equipment over the next eight years helping to double the company's annual turnover.

Helped by Business Link in the later development of new processes the company now took on board better quality products with Hi-Tech needs, this was matched by the installation of CAD (computer aided design) systems and the introduction of a new Health & Safety programme. Now in a strong position and with a much-respected name

Top left: A Doosan S550L in operation..
Above left: One of the newest machines in the firm, a SKQ 12 NC.
Left: Managing Director, Martin Birch.

Atkinsons - Success in Every Department

Is there anyone in Sheffield who, down the years, has not visited Atkinsons department store? In 2007 Atkinsons celebrated no less 135 years of service to the Sheffield public.

The firm was founded by John Atkinson who had arrived in Sheffield in 1865 to seek his fortune. At the age of 26, in 1872, after working as a sales representative, and with very little capital, John Atkinson launched his business from 90 South Street, Sheffield Moor dealing in lace, ribbons, and hosiery. From the outset he provided helpful service, good quality merchandise and value for money - the three ingredients of successful retailing.

By 1879 John Atkinson was so successful that his small shop was bursting at the seams and he took over two neighbouring shops, numbers 86 and 88.

Above: *Atkinsons 1902.*
Below: *The Golden Jubilee official photograph 1872-1922. John Atkinson is seated in the front row holding his umbrella.* **Below right:** *Store interior bedecked for Easter in 1923.*

Three shops were acquired in Prince Street in 1887 and opened as furniture showrooms, a new venture which John Atkinson plunged into with his customary business flair and drive.

Harold and Walter Atkinson soon joined the firm with the same dedication and enthusiasm as their father. A showroom for the shawl and mantle trade was opened behind Prince Street. Though growing in importance and prospering the business was however still basically six shops knocked into one and John Atkinson began to dream of the day when he would own his own department store.

The year of the big leap forward was 1892 when shops and land at 76-86 South Street were bought; five years later space at the back of 86 and 88 was bought and a new dress warehouse opened.

In 1901 the foundation stone was laid for an all-in-one store which was completed the following year. So many customers flocked to the store that a small army of assistants was needed to cope. John Atkinson's dream had been realised.

In 1975 the chairman, Walter Atkinson's son Peter, invited Sainsbury's to set up shop alongside his own; that £1,500,000 plan benefited both companies not least by providing a multi-storey car park.

The year 2000 saw the Atkinsons store expand by 50 per cent at the first floor level: the furniture area was doubled, more fashion concessions introduced along with an electrical department and a third restaurant.

Nothing stands still. The elevation facing Charter Row is now being redesigned to create a landmark building because of its prominence as the gateway to Sheffield's proposed New Retail Quarter.

Atkinsons continued to grow during the first world war, even though part of the premises were requisitioned as machine shops to produce war supplies. By 1918 further extensions were needed; ready-to-wear fashions were now playing a large part whilst the store had branched out to specialise in furs.

By the firm's golden jubilee in 1922, seven years before the founder's death, the store housed 46 departments.

Disaster struck in 1940. In December of that year the Germans launched their Blitz on Sheffield and in one night everything that the Atkinson family had built up over the previous 68 years was destroyed. Employees turning up for work the next day found nothing but rubble. Money left in the store had melted into a single mass.

But now Harold and Walter Atkinson showed their own flair for improvisation; within just a few weeks they opened for business again in temporary premises in St Judes Church and schoolroom in Milton street. The various departments were dispersed to premises at Johnson and Appleyard in Leopold Street, James Lamb on the Moor and even the Central Cinema. It was to be twenty years before the store could come together under one roof again.

Immediately after the war Atkinsons bought Tuckwoods high class grocers in Fargate which was turned into a department store and food hall with restaurant. In 1947 J.Walter Atkinson died; his brother Harold survived him by another eleven years, celebrating his fiftieth anniversary with the firm in 1954.

Atkinsons present Department Store on the Moor finally opened in 1960.

Today the fourth generation of the family in the shape of Nicholas Atkinson, great grandson of the founder, is at the helm of the Atkinson Group Ltd ensuring that what John Atkinson began in the 19th century is geared up to meet the challenges of the 21st.

Top left: *December 1940 after the Blitz.*
Left: *Peter Atkinson 1919-2004, Grandson of the founder.* ***Below:*** *An architects drawing of a re-vamped Charter Row elevation.*

The University of Sheffield - The Frontiers of Knowledge

Founded in 1905, but with roots going back to 1828, today the University of Sheffield has over 24,000 students from 116 countries and almost 6,000 staff.

The University has maintained and developed a reputation for world-class teaching and research excellence across a wide range of disciplines. Surveys carried out by Newsweek and China's Shanghai Jiao Tong University rank Sheffield among Britain's top 10 universities and the world's top 70.

Research partners and clients include Boeing, Rolls Royce, Unilever, Boots, AstraZeneca, GSK, ICI, and Slazenger, as well as UK and overseas government agencies and charitable foundations.

Academic partners include leading universities around the world. A partnership with Leeds and York Universities (the White Rose Consortium) has created a combined research resource greater than that of either Oxford or Cambridge.

A number of Queen's Anniversary prizes – most recently for research on ageing – have publicly recognised the University's significant contribution to the intellectual, economical, cultural and social life of the nation.

The University developed from three local institutions: the Sheffield School of Medicine, Firth College and the Sheffield Technical School.

The School of Medicine was founded 1828. Firth College was one of a group of university colleges developed out of

Above: The University buildings in 1905.
Right: The first year Chemistry laboratory before its transfer to the new building in 1953.

the Cambridge University Extension Movement, a scheme designed to bring university teaching to the towns and cities of England. Mark Firth, a local steel manufacturer established the College in 1879 for teaching Arts and Science.

The Sheffield Technical School was the product of the need for better technical training, particularly in steel-making. Established in 1884, in 1886 the School moved from Firth College to new premises on the site of the old Grammar School at St George's Square.

In 1897, the three institutions were amalgamated as the University College of Sheffield. On 31 May 1905 the University of Sheffield was granted its Royal Charter: that July the Firth Court Building on Western Bank was opened by King Edward VII and Queen Alexandra.

At the time there were 114 full-time students reading for degrees in Arts, Pure Science, Medicine and Applied Science.

During the first world war courses were available in munitions-making, medical appliances design and production, translation and politics. In 1919, when returning ex-servicemen were admitted, student numbers rose to a short-lived peak of about 1,000. By then the Faculty of Applied Science had split into Engineering and

In 2007 the spectacular £23 million Information Commons building, next to Brook Hill roundabout, opens to students. Complementing the existing library it promises to set a new standard for learning and study environments. More than a library, more than a study space, more than an IT centre, it will be a flexible 21st-century centre for many styles of group and individual learning and teaching, and the envy of other universities.

Recently, the University has seen a major expansion of its science and engineering facilities with the development of the new North Campus. A hub for multidisciplinary science and engineering, the campus includes two prestigious centres, the Kroto Research Institute and the Nanoscience and Technology Centre. The campus offers state-of-the-art facilities and support for high-tech businesses.

The University's new Student Village, based at current Endcliffe/Ranmoor sites, will provide state-of-the-art accommodation for students. The village will contain a full range of catering, retail, recreational and welfare facilities.

New and refurbished buildings at the old Jessop women's hospital will provide the latest facilities for some of the University's Arts and Humanities departments. The much-loved Victorian hospital building will be at the heart of a vibrant new centre on the University's campus.

Metallurgy; the University's first Hall of Residence (the original Stephenson Hall) had been established; and the Edgar Allen library had opened.

The University was equally committed to non-degree teaching: courses included cow-keeping, railway economics, mining and razor-grinding.

The second world war brought with it new areas of research and training - for example, radar, chemicals, magnetism, naval cartography and glass manufacture.

Post-war, many houses were brought into academic use and new buildings constructed - the Main Library in 1959, and the Arts Tower, Hicks Building, Alfred Denny Building, Sir Robert Hadfield Building, Chemical Engineering Building, University House, five Halls of Residence and the Union of Students in the 1960s.

New buildings for Geography and Psychology followed in the 1970s, along with the Crookesmoor Building (for Law and Management) and the Royal Hallamshire Hospital. The following decade saw the opening of the Octagon Centre and the Sir Henry Stephenson Building for engineering.

In the 1990s new premises for the School of Clinical Dentistry and the Management School were acquired. The Regent Court building, which houses the Departments of Computer Science and Information Studies and the Sheffield Centre for Health and Related Research, were also completed.

Top left: Views of the library, completed in 1959 (upper and lower left) and the new Information Commons building (upper and lower right). Above left: Three generations of University architecture: the original 1905 building was joined by the Arts Tower in 1965 and the Howard Florey building for Biomedical Science in 2004. Below: Vice-Chancellor Professor Bob Boucher receives the Queen's Anniversary Prize Gold Medal and Scroll in recognition of the University's contribution to the study of ageing and to improving the quality of life for older people.

SCX - Sheffield's X-factor

From its beginnings as a crane service and repair company, Sheffield's SCX Ltd has grown through four decades to become a market leader in specialist mechanical handling.

Keith Eastwood founded Street CraneXpress in 1972. Its first premises were next to the river Don on Clubmill Road, Sheffield. The business was originally formed as the service and repair division for Street Crane Company, providing maintenance services and repair work on factory cranes for local businesses.

The Clubmill Road premises were soon outgrown and in 1978 the business moved to a purpose-built factory and three small offices on its present site at Roman Ridge Road, just up the road from what is now the Meadowhall shopping centre.

In 1980, at the age of 18, Simon Eastwood, Keith Eastwood's son, joined Street CraneXpress.

Simon, a keen runner, scuba-diver and skier, had already completed a technician's course at the Engineering Industry Training Board. On joining Street CraneXpress Simon worked in each department before working full time in internal sales and administration.

In 1985 Street CraneXpress acquired Crane & Hoist Ltd which specialised in the supply of hoist units, jib cranes, gantries, slings and other materials handling equipment. Crane & Hoist was based on Parkway Close, but was now moved to the Roman Ridge site.

Newly qualifed as a Member of the Institute of Administrative Managers Simon Eastwood was placed in charge of Crane and Hoist, his brief to integrate it into the core business and expand it.

Simon took over the running of Street CraneXpress in its entirety in 1987. The company's first venture into a wider market came that year when it bought Burnand Components, an electrical wholesaler. Burnand was originally based on Shoreham Street, Sheffield. Burnand was very useful to Street CraneXpress since the company used the components Burnand supplied.

The Shoreham Street site was restricted, and so Burnand Components too was moved to the Roman Ridge site by taking over the paper factory next door.

During 1990, Burnand acquired XH Electric, a similar electrical distributor based in Hull. Two years later, a

further branch 'Burnand XH Components' was added in Scunthorpe.

In 1993 Intertotal Plc was launched, with a brief to win more technically

Top: Founder Keith Eastwood, 1976. Above right: Moving turf to close the access roads across Royal Ascot Racecourse. Right: SCX's Roman Ridge Road premises. Inset: The old paper factory acquired by the company to house Burnand Components.

up to do: bespoke mechanical handling work.

In 2000 Burnand XH bought Total Control Engineering, based in Hull, giving the group the distributor rights to a much wider range of electrical component brands.

SCX added an access division; manufacturing and maintaining building maintenance units in 2001.

In 2004 a new Street CraneXpress branch was set up in Bristol by buying out the branch from competitor Loadtite. This helped Street CraneXpress to better serve its customers in the South of England.

The following year SCX bought Integral Cradles Ltd, a London-based company involved in similar projects to SCX.

In 2006 the group was restructured with SCX Ltd as the name for the holding company of three subsidiaries: Street CraneXpress, Burnand XH and Integral Cradles.

Simon Eastwood has created a unique combination of mechanical handling services, products and solutions. Now with an annual turnover of £15m the family-owned company justifiably claims to be the UK's only 'true' supplier of a 'Total Solution To All Mechanical Handling Problems' - a remarkable achievement.

biased contracts. The new department would design, manufacture and install bespoke mechanical handling solutions for even the most unusual of requirements. Clients of this new division included the nuclear and aerospace industries, theatres, sports arenas and entertainment centres.

Intertotal Plc is today the Special Projects division of Street CraneXpress, undertaking many exciting and prestigious projects such as the moving turf to close the access roads across Royal Ascot Racecourse, an overhead gantry crane system for changing scenery and lighting at the Royal Opera House and the new moving roof for Wimbledon's Centre Court, due to be completed in 2009.

In 1997 Simon Eastwood gained an MBA from the University of Sheffield. That same year company growth exceeded all expectations, and the decision was made to merge Street CraneXpress, Crane & Hoist and Intertotal.

Street CraneXpress is made up of the Crane, Hoist and Service side of the business, continuing where the company began, offering maintenance, breakdown, refurbishment and repair services. The Special Projects Division, now undertakes the work that Intertotal was set

Top left: The overhead gantry crane system for changing scenery and lighting at the Royal Opera House.
Above left: The new retractable roof for Wimbledon's Centre Court, due to be completed in 2009.
Below: Simon Eastwood, Managing Director (right) and Kevin Walton, Director of Integral Cradles, at the signing of the merger in 2005.

Meadowhall - The Centre of Shopping

Ask the millions who drive past on the M1 what Sheffield is famous for and many will say 'steel'. But just as many will reply 'shopping'. Sheffield's national fame as a centre for shopping is down to one thing: Meadowhall.

Construction

Until 1984 the land on which Meadowhall stands was occupied by a steelworks owned by Hadfields Ltd.

When the steelworks closed, the land lay derelict until the construction of Meadowhall began. Before work could commence however, 100,000 cubic metres of contaminated waste had to be removed from the site. Construction began in June 1988 and took 27 months to complete. 2,500 construction jobs were created with some three quarters of those involved recruited locally.

Construction of Meadowhall included 2,000,000 bricks, 10,000 tons of steel, 98,000 cubic metres of concrete, 21,000 sq ft of glass and 10 miles of drainage pipes. There were 15,000 trees planted in and around the Centre.

Classical rather than contemporary architecture was utilised in the design and construction of Meadowhall to ensure it would never look dated.

Meadowhall Opens

Meadowhall finally opened its doors to customers at 10 am on Tuesday 4th September 1990 – on time and on budget!

By the end of the first morning over 50,000 people had visited the Centre, and ten days later Meadowhall's one millionth visitor walked through the doors. McDonald's served over 12,000 customers on the first day alone, smashing the company's previous record, and in the first week Pizza Hut actually sold out of food.

Around the Centre

In 1999 British Land bought Meadowhall from Stadium Developments for £1.17 billion, one of the largest property deals of all time. Meadowhall is British Land's biggest retail asset. British Land is one of the UK's largest property, management and investment companies. The company has an extensive portfolio, including shopping centres, retail parks and office property.

Meadowhall's malls are arranged into six areas each with a distinctive character and complementary mix of retailers. This 'retail mix' is constantly reviewed and many new names join the Centre each year.

High Street - the backbone of the Centre - offers shoppers all their favourite high street stores – a total of 95 units over two levels, including HMV, Gap, JJB Sports, Body Shop, Clinton Cards, banks and building societies anchored by Boots and WH Smith.

The Arcade - anchored by a Marks & Spencer flagship store - comprises 44 stores over two levels. Reminiscent of the grand Victorian arcades, the emphasis here is on fashion and accessories.

The Atrium is an extension to The Arcade, which links the malls directly to the Passenger Transport Interchange with its bus, train and Supertram services.

Park Lane is Meadowhall's most exclusive area. The mall is anchored by House of Fraser, Next and Debenhams. Traditional names including Crabtree & Evelyn, Laura Ashley and Jaeger share Park Lane with designer boutiques such as Karen Millen.

The Lanes is an exciting mix of individual, independent stores stocking a wide range of unique products - the perfect place to find unusual gifts.

Market Street features major high street names including Bhs, H&M, Argos Extra, Sports World, a large Mothercare and the Oasis Food Court - with its spectacular Mediterranean setting inspired by the famous Orange Square in Marbella.

The Oasis Food Court is one of the largest food courts in Europe, seating over 2,250 diners. The lower level offers a choice of quick service restaurants including Pizza Hut, KFC and McDonald's, as well as Nandos and La Tasca restaurants. On the upper level, there's a choice of continental cuisine from a range of waitress service restaurants, such as Mamma Amalfi, Margarita's, Pizza Express and Ma Potter's Chargrill. The Oasis Food Court, which underwent an £8 million refurbishment in 2003, is also home to an 11 screen cinema, giant video wall and a host of family entertainment.

The Source
In March 2003, 'The Source' at Meadowhall was officially opened. The 3,000 square metre flagship centre offers a fully equipped IT learning centre, conference facilities, employment services, research library, gym, aerobics studio and crèche.

The Future
Beginning in 2006 a £30 million mall refurbishment, the biggest in the Centre's history, was underway. It includes major improvements to the Centre architecture, lighting, air-conditioning, seating, escalators and signage - all aimed at creating an even better shopping experience for the Centre's shoppers.

Also underway is the £50 million configuration of Market Street, which will see new retailers, including Primark, arrive at the Centre - as well as the addition of 59,532 sq ft of retail space. Due to open in 2007, the new mall will help to create an even bigger 'Land of Shoppertunity'.

Left: *Construction of the the Dome.*
Below: *Meadowhall, Sheffield's 'Land of Shoppertunity'.*

ACKNOWLEDGMENTS

The publishers would like to thank

Local Studies Department, Sheffield Central Library
Andrew Mitchell
Steve Ainsworth

True North Books Ltd - Book List

Memories of Accrington - 1 903204 05 4

Memories of Barnet - 1 903204 16 X

Memories of Barnsley - 1 900463 11 3

More Memories of Barnsley - 1 903 204 79 8

Golden Years of Barnsley -1 900463 87 3

Memories of Basingstoke - 1 903204 26 7

Memories of Bedford - 1 900463 83 0

More Memories of Bedford - 1 903204 33 X

Golden Years of Birmingham - 1 900463 04 0

Birmingham Memories - 1 903204 45 3

More Birmingham Memories - 1 903204 80 1

Memories of Blackburn - 1 900463 40 7

More Memories of Blackburn - 1 900463 96 2

Memories of Blackpool - 1 900463 21 0

Memories of Bolton - 1 900463 45 8

More Memories of Bolton - 1 900463 13 X

Bolton Memories - 1 903204 37 2

Memories of Bournemouth -1 900463 44 X

Memories of Bradford - 1 900463 00 8

More Memories of Bradford - 1 900463 16 4

More Memories of Bradford II - 1 900463 63 6

Bradford Memories - 1 903204 47 X

Bradford City Memories - 1 900463 57 1

Memories of Bristol - 1 900463 78 4

More Memories of Bristol - 1 903204 43 7

Memories of Bromley - 1 903204 21 6

Memories of Burnley - 1 900463 95 4

Golden Years of Burnley - 1 900463 67 9

Memories of Bury - 1 900463 90 3

More Memories of Bury - 1 903 204 78 X

Memories of Cambridge - 1 900463 88 1

Memories of Cardiff - 1 900463 14 8

More Memories of Cardiff - 1 903204 73 9

Memories of Carlisle - 1 900463 38 5

Memories of Chelmsford - 1 903204 29 1

Memories of Cheltenham - 1 903204 17 8

Memories of Chester - 1 900463 46 6

More Memories of Chester -1 903204 02 X

Chester Memories - 1 903204 83 6

Memories of Chesterfield -1 900463 61 X

More Memories of Chesterfield - 1 903204 28 3

Memories of Colchester - 1 900463 74 1

Nostalgic Coventry - 1 900463 58 X

Coventry Memories - 1 903204 38 0

Memories of Croydon - 1 900463 19 9

More Memories of Croydon - 1 903204 35 6

Golden Years of Darlington - 1 900463 72 5

Nostalgic Darlington - 1 900463 31 8

Darlington Memories - 1 903204 46 1

Memories of Derby - 1 900463 37 7

More Memories of Derby - 1 903204 20 8

Memories of Dewsbury & Batley - 1 900463 80 6

Memories of Doncaster - 1 900463 36 9

More Memories of Doncaster - 1 903204 75 5

Nostalgic Dudley - 1 900463 03 2

Golden Years of Dudley - 1 903204 60 7

Memories of Edinburgh - 1 900463 33 4

More memories of Edinburgh - 1903204 72 0

Memories of Enfield - 1 903204 14 3

Memories of Exeter - 1 900463 94 6

Memories of Glasgow - 1 900463 68 7

More Memories of Glasgow - 1 903204 44 5

Memories of Gloucester - 1 903204 04 6

Memories of Grimsby - 1 900463 97 0

More Memories of Grimsby - 1 903204 36 4

Memories of Guildford - 1 903204 22 4

Memories of Halifax - 1 900463 05 9

More Memories of Halifax - 1 900463 06 7

Golden Years of Halifax - 1 900463 62 8

Nostalgic Halifax - 1 903204 30 5

Memories of Harrogate - 1 903204 01 1

Memories of Hartlepool - 1 900463 42 3

Memories of High Wycombe - 1 900463 84 9

Memories of Huddersfield - 1 900463 15 6

More Memories of Huddersfield - 1 900463 26 1

Golden Years of Huddersfield - 1 900463 77 6

Nostalgic Huddersfield - 1 903204 19 4

Huddersfield Memories - 1903204 86 0

Huddersfield Town FC - 1 900463 51 2

Memories of Hull - 1 900463 86 5

More Memories of Hull - 1 903204 06 2

Hull Memories - 1 903204 70 4

True North Books Ltd - Book List

Memories of Keighley - 1 900463 01 6
Golden Years of Keighley - 1 900463 92 X
Memories of Kingston - 1 903204 24 0
Memories of Leeds - 1 900463 75 X
More Memories of Leeds - 1 900463 12 1
Golden Years of Leeds - 1 903204 07 0
Memories of Leicester - 1 900463 08 3
Leeds Memories - 1 903204 62 3
More Leeds Memories - 1 903204 62 3
More Memories of Leicester - 1 903204 90 9
Memories of Leigh - 1 903204 27 5
Memories of Lincoln - 1 900463 43 1
Memories of Liverpool - 1 900463 07 5
More Memories of Liverpool - 1 903204 09 7
Liverpool Memories - 1 903204 53 4
More Liverpool Memories - 1 903204 88 7
Memories of Luton - 1 900463 93 8
Memories of Macclesfield - 1 900463 28 8
Memories of Manchester - 1 900463 27 X
More Memories of Manchester - 1 903204 03 8
Manchester Memories - 1 903204 54 2
More Manchester Memories - 1 903204 89 5
Memories of Middlesbrough - 1 900463 56 3
More Memories of Middlesbrough - 1 903204 42 9
Memories of Newbury - 1 900463 79 2
Memories of Newcastle - 1 900463 81 4
More Memories of Newcastle - 1 903204 10 0
Newcastle Memories - 1.903204 71 2
Memories of Newport - 1 900463 59 8
Memories of Northampton - 1 900463 48 2
More Memories of Northampton - 1 903204 34 8
Memories of Norwich - 1 900463 73 3
Memories of Nottingham - 1 900463 91 1
More Memories of Nottingham - 1 903204 11 9
Nottingham Memories - 1 903204 63 1
Bygone Oldham - 1 900463 25 3
Memories of Oldham - 1 900463 76 8
More Memories of Oldham - 1 903204 84 4
Memories of Oxford - 1 900463 54 7
Memories of Peterborough - 1 900463 98 9
Golden Years of Poole - 1 900463 69 5
Memories of Portsmouth - 1 900463 39 3
More Memories of Portsmouth - 1 903204 51 8
Nostalgic Preston - 1 900463 50 4
More Memories of Preston - 1 900463 17 2
Preston Memories - 1 903204 41 0
Memories of Reading - 1 900463 49 0

Memories of Rochdale - 1 900463 60 1
More Memories of Reading - 1 903204 39 9
More Memories of Rochdale - 1 900463 22 9
Memories of Romford - 1 903204 40 2
Memories of Rothertham- 1903204 77 1
Memories of St Albans - 1 903204 23 2
Memories of St Helens - 1 900463 52 0
Memories of Sheffield - 1 900463 20 2
More Memories of Sheffield - 1 900463 32 6
Golden Years of Sheffield - 1 903204 13 5
Sheffield Memories - 1 903204 61 5
More Sheffield Memories - 1 903204 91 7
More Leeds Memories - 1 903204 62 3
Memories of Slough - 1 900 463 29 6
Golden Years of Solihull - 1 903204 55 0
Memories of Southampton - 1 900463 34 2
More Memories of Southampton - 1 903204 49 6
Memories of Stockport - 1 900463 55 5
More Memories of Stockport - 1 903204 18 6
Stockport Memories - 1 903204 87 9
Memories of Stockton - 1 900463 41 5
Memories of Stoke-on-Trent - 1 900463 47 4
More Memories of Stoke-on-Trent - 1 903204 12 7
Memories of Stourbridge - 1903204 31 3
Memories of Sunderland - 1 900463 71 7
More Memories of Sunderland - 1 903204 48 8
Memories of Swindon - 1 903204 00 3
Memories of Uxbridge - 1 900463 64 4
Memories of Wakefield - 1 900463 65 2
More Memories of Wakefield - 1 900463 89 X
Nostalgic Walsall - 1 900463 18 0
Golden Years of Walsall - 1 903204 56 9
More Memories of Warrington - 1 900463 02 4
Warrington Memories - 1 903204 85 2
Memories of Watford - 1 900463 24 5
Golden Years of West Bromwich - 1 900463 99 7
Memories of Wigan - 1 900463 85 7
Golden Years of Wigan - 1 900463 82 2
More Memories of Wigan - 1 903204 82 8
Nostalgic Wirral - 1 903204 15 1
Wirral Memories - 1 903204 747
Memories of Woking - 1 903204 32 1
Nostalgic Wolverhampton - 1 900463 53 9
Wolverhampton Memories - 1 903204 50 X
Memories of Worcester - 1 903204 25 9
Memories of Wrexham - 1 900463 23 7
Memories of York - 1 900463 66 0